START AND RUN A PROFITABLE VIDEO STORE

A step-by-step business plan

Stan Loh

SELF-COUNSEL SERIES

International Self-Counsel Press Ltd. Self-Counsel Press Inc.
Vancouver Toronto Seattle

Printed in Canada

Copyright © 1983 by International Self-Counsel Press Ltd.
All rights reserved.

No part of this book may be reproduced or transmitted in any form by any means without permission in writing from the publisher, except by a reviewer who may quote brief passages in a review.

Printed in Canada

First edition: October, 1983

Cataloging in Publication Data:
Loh, Stan, 1942-
    Start and run a profitable video store

(Self-counsel series)
ISBN 0-88908-571-4

1. Home video systems industry — Canada. 2. Video recordings. I. Title.
II. Series.
HD9697.V543C35 1983   381'.4562138833   C83-091345-9

Cover design
    Sara Woodwark

658.022
L833

SELF-COUNSEL SERIES

International Self-Counsel Press Ltd.
Editorial Office
306 West 25th Street
North Vancouver
British Columbia V7N 2G1
Canada

Self-Counsel Press Inc.
1303 N. Northgate Way
Seattle
Washington, 98133 U.S.A.
(a subsidiary of International
Self-Counsel Press Ltd.)

To my wife and best friend
MABEL

CONTENTS

	INTRODUCTION	xiii
1	**A LITTLE BIT OF HISTORY**	1
2	**ARE YOU READY FOR THE VIDEO BUSINESS?**	3
	a. What kind of person makes a successful video dealer?	3
	b. How much money do you need?	3
	c. Where to raise the money	5
	d. What are you worth?	5
3	**YOUR MARKET AND LOCATION**	7
	a. The market	7
	b. Pay-TV and the market	7
	c. How to select your location	8
	1. Strip centers	8
	2. Freestanding stores	8
	3. Mall locations	8
	4. Places to avoid	9
	d. The size of your store	9
	e. Your store name	10
	f. Your signs	11
4	**START-UP CONSIDERATIONS**	13
	a. Your lease	13
	b. Business registration license	13
	c. Sales tax registration	13
	d. Utilities and telephones	14
	e. Cash registers	14
	f. Charge cards	14
	g. Printing	15
	h. Security	15
	1. Store security	16
	2. Security on your movies	16
	i. Planning your floor space	16
5	**YOUR OPERATING BUDGET**	21
6	**WHAT TYPE OF BUSINESS STRUCTURE SHOULD YOU CHOOSE?**	25
	a. A proprietorship	25
	b. A partnership	25
	c. Corporations	26
	d. Franchise operations	27

7	**HIRING YOUR PERSONNEL**	**29**
	a. Finding good staff	29
	b. The job description	32
	c. Screening and interviewing	32
	d. Job schedules	34
8	**STOCKING YOUR STORE**	**35**
	a. Selecting a distributor	35
	b. Take advantage of sales terms	36
	1. Net 30 days	36
	2. 5%, 30 days	37
	3. 2%, 10 days, net 30 days	37
	4. 2%, 10th following month	37
	5. Dating	37
	6. Shipping terms	38
	c. Floor plan purchases	38
9	**YOUR CHOICE OF STOCK**	**41**
	a. Hardware	41
	b. Accessories	42
	c. VHS versus Beta	42
	1. The differences	43
	2. Making your choice	43
	3. Market trends	44
	d. The disk formats	45
	e. How many to buy?	46
	f. Choosing good movies	47
	g. The movie register	48
	h. Organizations that can help	49
10	**THE NEW AGE AND VIDEO RETAILING**	**51**
	a. Video games	51
	1. Video game rentals	52
	2. Video game consumers	52
	3. Video game buying	52
	b. Computers	53
	c. Satellite TV	53
11	**RENTAL SYSTEMS**	**57**
	a. Movies	57
	1. Vid-shelves	57
	2. The movie board	59
	3. Behind the counter	59
	4. Space saver merchandiser	60
	5. Catalogues	60
	6. Library rental cases	61
	7. Pre-viewing rentals	61

	b.	Machine rentals	62
		1. Regular rental	62
		2. Rent to buy	62
	c.	Deposits on rentals	63

12 MEMBERSHIP PLANS — 65
  a. Advantages — 65
  b. Disadvantages — 65
  c. Membership privileges — 65
  d. The membership card — 66
  e. Movie reservations — 67

13 ADVERTISING AND PROMOTION — 69
  a. Advertising — 69
     1. Newspapers — 70
     2. Magazines — 70
     3. Radio — 70
     4. Television — 70
     5. Yellow pages — 71
     6. Co-op advertising — 71
     7. Mailing list — 71
     8. Advertising program — 72
  b. Promotion — 72
     1. Grand opening — 72
     2. Commander board — 73
     3. "Ladies," "senior citizens" or "members" night — 73
     4. 99¢ deal — 73
     5. Kids' deals — 73
     6. Birthday deals — 74
     7. The new arrival board — 74
     8. Posters — 74
     9. Staff's choice — 74
     10. Newsletters — 76
     11. Special effects — 76
     12. Special events — 77
     13. Change displays — 77

14 MARKETING YOUR VIDEO STORE — 79
  a. Selling — 79
  b. How to demonstrate video equipment — 80
     1. Know the product — 80
     2. Explain the product — 80
     3. Show the product — 80
     4. Ask the customer — 81
     5. Close the sale — 81
  d. Follow-ups — 82

15	**DAILY OPERATIONS**	**83**
a.	Hours of operation	83
b.	Good housekeeping	83
c.	Cutting costs	84
d.	Daily sales summary	84
e.	Cash reconciliation	86
f.	Banking	86
g.	Accounting	86
16	**EVALUATING AND SELLING YOUR VIDEO STORE**	**89**
a.	Valuation methods	89
b.	How to forecast sales	90
c.	Risk and return on investment	91
d.	How to value a video store by capitalizing future earnings	91
e.	How to value your store on the basis of asset appraisal	92
	1. Assets	92
	2. Goodwill	92
	3. Inventory	92
f.	The final offer	94
h.	After the price is established	95

APPENDIX 1
The 200 most popular movies — 96

APPENDIX 2
Recommended magazines and books — 101

LIST OF SAMPLES

#1	Financial statement	6
#2	Budget	21
#3	Estimated gross profits	22
#4	Expense budget	22
#5	Budgetary planning and performance review process	23
#6	Job description questionnaire	30
#7	Application form	32
#8	Membership card	58
#9	Movie check list	58
#10	Machine rental form	64
#11	Daily sales summary	85

ACKNOWLEDGMENTS

In writing this book, I had the good fortune to be assisted by a number of people.

Thanks to all the video dealers and suppliers across the North American continent — they have been a great inspiration to me.

Almost daily help was given to me by my wife, Mabel, throughout the entire period during which the book was being written. Thanks also to Bill McCartney, Uwe Schnack, and Bill Bouvette who have contributed so much to this book — and to my life. And to Diane Chan who volunteered so unselfishly to type the major portion of the manuscript over the Christmas of 1982.

INTRODUCTION

In 1975 the Sony Corporation introduced a video home recorder called Betamax that sparked off a new and exciting business throughout the world. This business has generated thousands of new jobs. Manufacturers of the equipment employ skilled technicians, distributors hire sales people, retailers employ sales and administrative staff, and duplicators hire warehouse workers and technicians.

The video business has, in a very short while, become the hottest industry in the world. In North America, where entertainment at home has long been very popular, thousands of video retail outlets sell equipment and services, rent movies and mass merchandise video games, and push computers and the like.

According to experts in the business, sales will exceed one billion dollars by 1985. And, according to *Billboard*, a well-known music and house entertainment newspaper, sales may reach the one trillion dollar mark by 1990.

In the U.S., figures show that in the first part of 1982 sales of video cassette recorders (VCRs) jumped 600,000 units to more than 3.8 million units. There are about 300,000 units currently in Canada and that rate is growing 20% per year.

Every month you see new developments in the video business, and every day it seems a new outlet is opening somewhere. It has been estimated that there are no less than 50,000 outlets of various combinations in North America.

Running a video business can be fun, but it is not for the weak-hearted. The business, like any that is hot, has become cutthroat and extremely competitive. It is also a very complex business with intrigues in marketing strategy, quality control problems, poor margins, piracy and so on. To complicate matters further, there are myriad formats to make decisions on, many variations of rental schemes, lease programs, and a hundred and one promotions needed to succeed. The hours are long and at times tedious.

Still, if you have a good financial background and have some money stored away that can be rolled into the business, you can generate a good profit and, as I stated earlier, you can get some fun out of it.

If you think you can cash in on the business in a very short time, I suggest you look elsewhere. It takes a long time to recoup your capital and the pay out period can be a long and hard one. Being a video retailer also takes a lot of business know-how.

This book will guide the video retailer in daily operations. It will discuss various ways to run the business, how to run a movie club, how to choose your format, what to look for when hiring personnel, and what to ask for if you sell the business.

In short, this book will give you a good retail business background and let you have an edge over your competition.

1
A LITTLE BIT OF HISTORY

The history of video dates back to the late nineteenth century when televisions were first thought of. However, home video was only thought of seven to eight years ago.

George Carey suggested in 1875 in Boston that a system should be made to rapidly scan each element of a picture in succession, line by line and frame by frame. This idea was subsequently developed and it established the possibility of using only a single wire or channel for transmission. In 1873 Paul Nipkow submitted a patent in Germany for a complete television system, and in 1908 A. Campbell Swinton outlined a method that is the basis of modern television. He proposed the use of cathode-ray tubes magnetically deflected at both camera and receiver. Many other inventors improved on the early television since then.

Television networks throughout the world have used the bulky and clumsy video tape recorders since 1956. These are very costly, but during those early days they were a great improvement over the time when everything programmed had to be live. Now programs may be filmed well beforehand, and edited and spliced together.

Few people, even in Japan, remember the Tokyo Telecommunications Engineering Corporation. But 30 years ago it was a young company with a good idea: the magnetic reel to reel audio tape recorder. This company changed its name to Sony Corporation, and the rest is history.

In 1967 Sony introduced the first portable, low-cost black and white video tape recorder (VTR) and camera to the television industry. At last television camera crews could film outside studios on location. They now can take cameras everywhere.

Gradually this recorder made its way to cable television stations, schools, and smaller television studios. However, the VTR was still primitive. It was a reel to reel type where one reel of film was drawn through a system of transports into another open spool. It was cumbersome and bulky, and the reels were heavy and created a lot of problems for the operators. Camera crews found the load too heavy to carry for long periods of time.

In 1972 Sony introduced a vast improvement to the whole system. It brought out the first video cassette recorder (VCR). The one inch reel was now compacted into a three-quarter inch cassette. One-hour programs could be recorded onto one cassette. Television stations made wholesale conversion of all their reel programs to cassette recorders because storage and library cataloging was easier and took less space.

Still the cassette recorder was too bulky for home use. Researchers tried hard to reduce the VCR to a smaller size and yet keep costs down so that it would be more affordable. At last in 1975 Sony introduced Betamax, the first home video cassette recorder.

This was the signal that all American home owners were waiting for. The response was so good that the first shipment from Japan was sold out prior to reaching the American stores. Other manufacturers scrambled to produce their own VCRs and raced to capture the billions of dollars that was going to be spent all over the world on VCRs.

2
ARE YOU READY FOR THE VIDEO BUSINESS?

a. WHAT KIND OF PERSON MAKES A SUCCESSFUL VIDEO DEALER?

People from all walks of life have started their own video business. I know accountants, pilots, sales people, municipal clerks, and laborers who have become video operators. And of course there are the graduates from the electronics and broadcasting business, the recording business, and those that are closely or remotely related to the motion picture business.

These people share one good quality. They are adventurous and willing to take risks. They are also usually not very conservative. They are willing to attempt something that is new to them.

One other very important quality these people share is that they are hardworking. This is something that cannot be taught — it comes from motivation. The motivation is mainly money or profits. The hope is that profits generated from the business will exceed the sacrifices that you will have to make.

As a video operator, you will soon find out that the hours of operation will keep you away from home for long hours. Some people solve this problem by involving their spouses in the business. In many cases this has turned out well, but in other cases the marriage was the victim of constant contact. If you and your spouse can stand each other's moods and whims 24 hours a day, that is a good sign. If not, do not involve your spouse full time in your store.

You also have to like meeting people — all sorts of people. This quality can be developed. I have seen very shy and nervous operators develop into first class business people over the counter. Lastly, you have to like being in the movie business. There is no point going into the video business if you don't enjoy talking about it with your customers.

b. HOW MUCH MONEY DO YOU NEED?

Before you can figure out how much money you need, you have to decide what kind of store you want, and how big an operation you need. The following example will give you an idea of the different financial considerations.

Let us assume that you want a medium size store that runs about 1100 square feet. You also want a movie club, and you want to rent and sell machines. Also included in your shopping list are an assortment of accessories.

Your budget might look like this:

ITEM	COST RANGE $		
Rent (first and last months)	2,200	—	3,000
Renovations and decor	5,000	—	7,000
Equipment			
(10 for rent)	7,000	—	10,000
(10 for sale)	7,000	—	10,000
Movies			
(400 titles VHS only)	24,000	—	28,000
(200 titles Beta only)	12,000	—	14,000
Accessories	700	—	1,000
Rental cases	800	—	1,000
Signage and cash register	3,000	—	4,300
Utility and telephone deposits	500	—	1,000
Legal fees and registration	500	—	700
Security	1,000	—	1,500
Insurance	1,500	—	1,800
Printing	500	—	600
Pre-opening labor (3 persons)	3,000	—	4,000
Miscellaneous	1,000	—	2,000
	69,700	—	89,900
Suggested operating capital	+ 12,000	—	17,000
TOTAL	81,700	—	106,900

Of course there will be variations in every case. The above is only a guide to making your budget. Some equipment like your cash register and neon signs may be leased instead of bought. You may decide not to have the Beta format in your store. Your movie inventory can be trimmed or increased. But remember, gone are those days when this business can be started up with 300 titles — there is simply too much competition.

In 1982 the average wholesale dollar value of inventory during the slowest season was $120,230.* It rose to $176,830 during the peak season. These figures show about a 90% increase over 1981 figures.

The average gross sales by product were:

	1981	1980
Hardware	48%	44%
Software	31%	26%
Accessories	10%	12%
Service	19%	18%

---

*1982 video retailer survey, *The Video Store*.

In the preceding example, 27% of the budget was in equipment and 71% in movies. This indicates that this store is more a movie video store than the typical video store that also sells lots of equipment. A major proportion of income would come from the rental of movies rather than from sales of equipment.

c. WHERE TO RAISE THE MONEY

Once you determine how much money you need, you have to raise the funds.

The first place to look is in your own pocket. What savings do you have? What can you sell to make liquid cash? Do you have an old piano in the basement that you have not touched for a long time? That may be worth a couple of thousand. How about the bonds you purchased six years ago? Can you cash them in? Or the term deposit that is up for renewal?

One of the biggest investments of your lifetime may be your home. There is equity in it and you may want to apply for a second mortgage from your bank.

Another cheap source of funds is your insurance company. If you have had life insurance for several years, chances are you can borrow some money against your policy at a much lower rate of interest than what financial institutions can offer.

Whatever you do I would strongly recommend you *not* go to loan sharks for funds. Your troubles will be endless. Make sure the financial companies you borrow money from are legitimate financial institutions — banks, trust companies, credit unions. When you go for a mortgage, always have your own legal advice. The few hundred dollars you spend will be well worth it. There are many clauses in a mortgage agreement that the average person does not understand or even read. Your lawyer does that for you. I am warning you: *do not sign your house and life savings away.*

If you are still short of funds, you could borrow from relatives or close friends. If you do borrow from friends, make sure their money goes to good use or you might lose them as friends altogether.

One thing to keep in mind when borrowing from friends and relatives is to lay down the ground rules. They may take advantage of your financial or moral obligation. Tell them that you will pay them interest at the market rate and that if they want to purchase goods from your store, you will treat them specially although you still have to make a profit to cover overhead. After all, they are lending you money at a profit. Put any agreement you have in writing, and get legal advice first.

d. WHAT ARE YOU WORTH?

Before you go to a banker, make sure you prepare a statement of your financial standing. The more prepared you are, the better chance you have of obtaining a positive answer about the loan you want.

To see how your financial statement should look, see Sample #1. I urge you to review this statement periodically just to know where you stand.

SAMPLE #1
FINANCIAL STATEMENT

WHAT YOU OWN

Cash
Cash on hand $ _____
Checking account $ _____
Savings account $ _____
Money market funds $ _____
Term deposits $ _____
Life insurance cash value $ _____
Money owed to you $ _____
     Total $ _____

Marketable Securities
Stocks $ _____
Bonds $ _____
Government securities $ _____
Mutual funds $ _____
Other investments $ _____
     Total $ _____

Personal property
Automobiles $ _____
Household furnishings $ _____
Jewelry and collectibles $ _____
Others $ _____
     Total $ _____

Real Estate
Homes $ _____
Other properties $ _____
     Total $ _____

Pension
Vested portion of
 company plan $ _____
Vested benefits $ _____
Private retirement plans $ _____
Government pension plans $ _____
Others $ _____
     Total $ _____

Long Term Assets
Equity in business $ _____
Life insurance $ _____
Annuities $ _____
     Total $ _____

  GRAND TOTAL $ _____

WHAT YOU OWE

Current Bills
Rent $ _____
Utilities $ _____
Charge accounts $ _____
Credit cards $ _____
Insurance premiums $ _____
Alimony $ _____
Child support $ _____
Others $ _____
     Total $ _____

Taxes
Federal $ _____
Provincial or
 state $ _____
Local $ _____
Taxes on
 investments $ _____
Others $ _____
     Total $ _____

Mortgages
Homes $ _____

Other properties $ _____
     Total $ _____

Debts to individuals $ _____
     Total $ _____

Loans
Automobiles $ _____
Education $ _____
Home improvement $ _____
Life insurance $ _____
Others $ _____
     Total $ _____

  GRAND TOTAL $ _____

SUMMARY
Grand Total of What You Own $ _____
Less Grand Total of What You
         Owe $ _____
     NET WORTH $ _____

3
YOUR MARKET AND LOCATION

a. THE MARKET

Statistics show that there are at least 1.3 televisions per household. Experts say that VCR sales will not be as good as televisions for the first few years, but sales will be impressive as the price declines. VCRs offer an alternative to costly nights out for most families. Going to the cinema can cost a family of four about $20 not including popcorn, parking, and gas. A movie rental averages $4. What a saving!

Statistically, the average VCR owner is between 25 and 50, and married with an income of about $20,000 a year or more. Most VCR owners hold steady jobs. They are executives, factory workers, bankers, doctors, professionals, civil servants, etc.

b. PAY-TV AND THE MARKET

In Canada, where Pay-TV is still in its infancy, the effect of it on the video business is too far off to be assessed. Canadian license holders have been ordered by the CRTC (Canadian Radio - Television & Telecommunications Commission) to devote 45% of revenues in each year to Canadian productions. The problem is getting money to fund these productions — a case of the chicken or the egg. A base of a large subscribing but paying public is still needed.

In the U.S. Pay-TV has had a few years under its belt and it has not made any dents on the video business. This is due to the low percentage of homes hooked up to cable. However, about 250,000 homes are added on to cable monthly and more cable services are started in American cities yearly.

In Hawaii, where many channels of Pay-TV have been available for a good number of years, video stores are still actively soliciting business everywhere.

Towns in remote areas that are plagued by poor TV reception and little choice of channels now have an alternative. Likewise, these rural areas will have problems getting Pay-TV because Pay-TV is linked with cable systems that do not reach these areas.

Consider also that nearly 40,000 American and Canadian homes have small individual satellite earth stations capable of pulling in more than 50 Pay-TV and cable program services. Most of these 40,000 earth stations have VCRs as part of the equipment which in turn will create revenue in accessory sales and movie rentals.

About 3.5 million North American homes now have VCRs and related equipment. Sales in the first quarter of 1982 were an overwhelming 40% higher than the same quarter of 1981.

These figures prove one thing — the video business is far from being endangered by Pay-TV. In fact, according to RCA, the industry is merely beginning.

The advantage of VCR is versatility and choice. While cable and satellite and regular television programming offer a huge range of entertainment, the VCR offers alternatives. With your VCR you can record any program you want and watch it at any time you want.

c. HOW TO SELECT YOUR LOCATION

After analyzing your market size, it is time to look for your location. You have a choice between a strip center, mall location, or a free-standing store. Look for space that is located on a major street.

1. Strip centers

Strip centers are sometimes referred to as plazas. Many of them have been redevelopments of old service station sites at major intersections. Strip centers are an American and Canadian commercial real estate phenomena. They usually consist of a small number of stores sharing a single building. They are unlike malls because entrance to each store is from the outside.

These plazas have a few advantages over freestanding video stores. Other tenants in the plaza can be a good draw for your store. Ample parking is usually available. If there is a bank in the plaza, it will be an advantage — people who leave a bank usually have a few dollars to spend.

An all-night or 24 hour grocery store in the plaza also helps. The operating hours will bring exposure to your store, and will also provide good security.

2. Freestanding stores

Freestanding stores are self-explanatory. You are in total control of the parking, advertising, etc. Be very careful about the security of your store if it is freestanding. Make sure you have a good security company looking after you.

3. Mall locations

About 4% of video stores are located in an enclosed mall.

I feel that mall locations have been untested for video outlets. The potential may be tremendous simply based on the sheer numbers of people that frequent malls where parking is not a problem. But one big drawback is the rent in mall locations. Rent usually ranges from $10 to $18 per square foot. A plaza or strip center location costs about $6 to $8 per square foot. Also, some mall managements charge a percentage of gross profits on top of basic rent as well as charging for housekeeping and mall administration.

In a mall location, your hours of operation are tied in with mall hours. This may pose a problem for the return of movies. Often mall entrances are closed early in the morning which means that customers cannot drop off movies through letter slots like they can in freestanding or strip center stores. In some regions, you cannot open on holidays and Sundays, which are pretty good sales days in this business.

4. Places to avoid

Based on retail development studies conducted by Exxon in the early 1970s for service station sites, it was discovered that automobile owners purchased gas more often on their way home rather than on their way to work. The same holds true for video store rentals. If you are selecting your location in a strip center or freestanding store, choose one on the side of the major street that leads most workers home from work, and avoid, if possible, a street where a median divider may cut your traffic in half.

You should also avoid major intersections where traffic jams are liable to occur. If traffic is too heavy, drivers dislike pulling off and later fighting their way back into the traffic line.

Another good place to avoid is where there is a large road network. Such places are already a confusion for drivers. They do not need a video store to add to the confusion.

If your area has a good mix of professionals, executives, blue collar workers, singles, and students, you are probably in a prime location. If the surrounding area has a good mixture of apartments, single dwelling units and townhouses, that is a good sign.

You can get up-to-date figures on numbers of households and the population mix from your local Chamber of Commerce. Municipal halls and libraries may also have this information.

Remember, however, that the success of your operation depends on the number of VCR owners more than the population. If you want a better feel for the market, don't hesitate to call on local television and video stores and ask the dealers how their sales of VCRs have been.

d. THE SIZE OF YOUR STORE

One important market and location consideration is the size of your store. This will depend on a couple of major factors. The first is your available funds. Do you have enough to have a large video store? If not, can you raise the funds? The second is your ability to run a large store. Do you want to run a large store and have the problems that go with a large store?

Before you even consider a long term lease, you should reconsider the type of store you wish it to be. What do you want to sell or rent in it? Do you want to have a huge movie club? Do you want to rent as well as sell VCRs, accessories, cameras, video games, and computers? How many movie titles do you wish to have in five years? Displaying movie titles is a major concern of your movie club. And they can take up a lot of wall and floor space.

A couple of years ago, you could open a video store that had 500 movie selections, and rented and sold VCRs at about a rate of 30 units a month. That meant you needed a maximum of 1,000 square feet.

Today, that floor area will be too small. Five hundred titles is quite a small figure to begin a store with if your store is located in a metropolitan area. If you are in a rural setting, where competition is less, you could possibly get by with 500 titles. In an ordinary store, count on having about 1,500 square feet. Give yourself some room to play around with in planning your floor space for merchandising. You do not want to feel shut in. Customers like an airy atmosphere.

You should get a plan drawn to actual scale and include in the plan all you want to see in your store. Consider your movie area, your equipment display area and your accessories. In short, a lot of planning will be necessary before you sign your lease. Of course, the larger the space you need, the higher the rent will be. Make sure you can be comfortable paying the rent every month of your lease. However, do distinguish rent from location. The higher the rent does not mean the better the location.

Also, do not forget that moving to a bigger location just because you ran out of space can be very expensive. Moving is expensive. Costs are incurred because of renovations, new fixtures, address changes, sign and printing costs, and administration costs. More important, you might lose business because there will be some customers who will not drive to your new location for one reason or another. If you move, you also face the danger of someone leasing your old place and subsequently stealing some of your old customers.

When you look for a location and space, do not lease one that is too big for your needs. If you are going to use 1,800 square feet out of 3,000 square feet, your store is going to look pretty bare. It will look like you are underfinanced and do not have enough stock to sell. If you have excess space you are paying excess rent.

e. YOUR STORE NAME

The name of your store will probably be one of the first thoughts in your mind. It is like naming your first born; you want to give it a nice sounding name and, at the same time, a catchy one that people will remember.

Start by putting names down on a piece of paper. Get your partners (if any) to do the same. Even your relatives and friends can be involved. Give them a week to come up with a dozen names each. At the end of the week, sit down with everyone and have a brainstorming session. You will be surprised how good your colleagues are in coming up with great names for your store.

After shortlisting your names to half a dozen or so, discuss each one of them. Toss out those that might offend anyone. Eliminate names that are difficult to say. Tongue twisters and long names are hard to remember.

Your store should have some straightforward reference to the business you are in. For example you will not want to call your store "Jack Jones and Company Ltd." because that does not refer to the kind of business you are in.

Whatever names you come up with, keep the last six in reserve. In most regions, you are allowed to submit three names, in order of preference, to the state or province for registration. Your lawyer can help you in your submission and registration. Sometimes personally calling the Companies Office in your state or province can help speed up the process of obtaining a name for your store. If you are intending to expand, you will do well to register your store name nationwide as soon as possible. That will eliminate other contenders and avoid future problems.

Now that you have got a name, keep repeating it. Get it in your head, and your staff's, that the name must be broadcasted. Get a sign made, and hang it on your storefront.

f. YOUR SIGNS

As soon as you have decided on the name of your store and are sure you want to live with it for a long time, get it registered. The registration will take quite a while before you get a final approval. Upon approval, design a permanent storefront sign if you have already signed the lease for your place.

Most municipalities today have strict guidelines or by-laws concerning storefront signs. For example, some will no longer allow protruding neon or other signs from buildings because they can be a traffic hazard. Ask your local authorities what the restrictions are in your area.

Most plans for signs will have to be submitted to municipalities for approval along with any major internal building renovations. Most sign companies have personnel to help you draw up plans and composite color drawings. Municipalities are also very fussy about the quality of the sign you plan to erect.

One store that I know had their store opening delayed because of bureaucratic delays in the sign approval. The planners made the store owner submit four separate sets of plans for the sign. They were very slow in making suggestions when each plan was rejected. The sign was finally approved after three months. In the end, the owner had to change the color of the sign even though all the other stores in the chain had an established house color.

Try to budget enough time so that a temporary sign doesn't have to be put up when the store opens. A temporary sign doesn't give the store a very good start, and it reflects a lack of professionalism. But if you are anxious enough to open your store for business, a temporary sign versus other problems may not be a big deal.

4
START-UP CONSIDERATIONS

a. YOUR LEASE

When looking for a lease, you might want to ask the help of a real estate sales person to do some hunting for you. You will have to tell him or her what you require for a good location. Usually real estate people have a pretty good idea what is available in their locality. They also know what the going rates are including the ins and outs of most types of leases. This service is free to you as the buyer or lessee. Only the seller or lessor pays a real estate commission.

When negotiating a lease, try to get one that will give you a three year term with an option to renew for another three at the end of it. Of course, you should try to negotiate for a lower rent.

A three-year lease is long enough for you to benefit from the improvements you made to the site and not so long that you are stuck when you are ready to move to a bigger or better location.

If you are leasing a free-standing location, and if you are going to have to put in a sizeable amount of money to develop it, try to get an option to purchase the property as well. This is to protect yourself just in case your landlord decides to sell. Although you are tied in with a lease, you do not want to be told to leave at the end of your term — assuming your business is going well. Moving, as I said earlier, is expensive. Of course, if you need more space, you will want to move.

b. BUSINESS REGISTRATION LICENSE

All businesses need to be registered, and business licenses must be issued by local governments. Your city hall will have information on how this is done. The fees are usually not very high, but do not forget to budget for them.

c. SALES TAX REGISTRATION

If you are in a region where sales tax applies, make sure you register immediately. Knowing the slow speed of bureaucratic procedures, I would be surprised if you got it back before you opened your store.

The registration is necessary for your store. In some regions, you must charge the applicable tax on each purchase. In other words, you are the tax collector for your region. At the end of each month you are required to complete the applicable forms and remit the taxes collected. If you forget this important chore, you may end up being audited.

d. UTILITIES AND TELEPHONES

Telephone and utility service should be applied for early. You don't want to run the risk of not having telephone communication on opening day.

Telephone connections are usually slow in most cities, but they are vital to your business. Sometimes alarm systems are tied in with the telephone systems, which means the telephones must go in before the security system.

You must decide how many lines you require and where the telephones should be located. Plan with foresight. In your type of business you will not require toll free lines. They are costly, so save the expense.

e. CASH REGISTERS

When shopping for a cash register (either to purchase or to lease) take special care not to spend too much. You will want one that can accommodate all the categories of sales or rentals you have. Here are some major categories as a guide:

(a) Hardware

(b) Movie rentals

(c) Equipment rentals

(d) Accessories

(e) Miscellaneous

The reason for having categorized sales is to give you an idea of sales of certain categories of products. This will help you in your buying later on. Most cash registers have at least five categories for ringing up a sale. If you have other categories, you will need a cash register that will give you more capabilities.

With the advent of computers in business, especially in small business, computerized cash registers have made it into the video industry. Such cash registers will provide loads of information, save on labor, and cut your paperwork. If you have spare cash in your budget, this is one item you should consider leasing or buying.

f. CHARGE CARDS

In North America, the power of the major charge or credit cards over both merchant and the consumer is overwhelming. Most people own at least one credit card and most businesses accept them.

Your store should have merchant accounts with the more popular credit cards — VISA and MasterCard, at least. Contact your local offices early because it takes some time to set up an account.

You should know that the credit card companies or banks will charge you a percentage of your gross charge sales. The percentage varies according to the amount of sales. A low sales figure of, say, $2,000 a month could mean you would pay as much as 5% to the credit card company.

g. PRINTING

There will be a good amount of printing to be done when you start your business. Here are some of the jobs that will need doing:

(a) Invoices

(b) Receipts

(c) Business cards

(d) Lease agreements

(e) Handouts

(f) Advertising flyers

(g) Membership cards

(h) Movie catalogues

Because you will do quite a bit of printing, it is a good idea to shop around for a reputable yet economical printer. Meet with the manager of several printing companies and ask for terms and prices.

h. SECURITY

1. Store security

Once you have leased the store, there are many things to do other than rent movies. One important thing to do is to arrange for security of the store.

There are many security companies that can take care of you. It would be wise to call at least three companies to give you advice and estimates.

One thing you cannot afford to have is a cheap burglar alarm system. Video and drug stores get hit most often by burglars.

The best systems to have are those that detect intrusion and motion combined. The alarm that is linked to a police station is best, but these days it is impossible for a small video store to buy these services. The next best thing is to get one that is linked up to a security office that provides 24 hour service. Should there be a break-in, the alarm is triggered at the security office who in turn call the police. The reaction is pretty swift. Usually the message gets through to a patrol car within two to three minutes.

In those two or three minutes you want to deter the thieves from doing any damage. You might install presentable looking bars in the front of your store where there is glass. Do not forget the door if it is also made of glass. If you have a back door, ensure it has good locks. Deadbolt locks are best.

In addition, examine your doors. Make sure they have the right hinges. Often doors have hinges that can be undone from the outside with a simple screwdriver and hammer. If you find these in your premises, negotiate with your landlord to have better doors.

One cheap way to cure this problem (if you do not want to spend money on new doors) is to screw in, on the inside of the hinge, a metal screw. This will prevent the hinge from being undone from the outside.

If you have a burglar alarm that detects motion, you cannot allow your customers the privilege of returning your movies through the mail slot. However, returning movies through the mail slot is not such a good idea anyway. It is really quite easy to steal movies from the mail slot using a coat hanger.

2. Security on your movies

You will find that there are crooks who will steal your original movies. They make a copy using two VCRs and keep the original. Of course, the original has a better picture quality than the duplicated one. Switching cassette shells and labels isn't difficult for a determined thief.

To prevent crooks from doing this, purchase labels for your cassettes that are difficult to lift and replace. Stick these labels on both sides of the cassette. After a few minutes it will be impossible to take the label off without damaging it. If peeled off, the label should say "Void." Your wholesalers should have these labels in stock.

Some dealers prefer to stick the labels around the two rear corners of the cassette. This makes it more difficult to lift the security label off. Where you stick your labels is entirely your choice, but make sure you have security labels.

Crooks are everywhere. They may even be your competitors. What is there to stop them from buying the labels from your wholesaler and cheating you?

Look for a wholesaler who has a register that records by number the dealer who purchased the labels.

This is a cheap way to prevent movie losses. Labels cost about 10¢ each. If you lose one movie, you have lost the cost of 1,000 labels.

There are also more expensive ways to prevent movie losses. Some outfits use ultra-violet detectors with fluorescent paint on the hubs and spot paint on the back of the movie tape. When the movie is returned it is placed under this light. If there is paint on the hubs and tape the movie is yours. If not, a copy has been made.

Remember, marking the shell doesn't help; the crooks want the movie tape, not the container.

i. PLANNING YOUR FLOOR SPACE

No matter what size store you have leased, you must use all available floor and wall space to maximize profit. You do not need professional help in doing this. Interior decorators and architects will only increase your cost. If you feel you need advice, seek the help of students in your local technical or architectural college. Usually, these students have up-to-date and challenging ideas.

If you plan the store yourself, make sure you make several plans, and seek second and third opinions.

You want to make your store comfortable and welcoming, yet you want to avoid making it so comfortable that customers stay all day watching your display movies free of charge. You will find, as a retailer, that all retail stores have a few customers who will come into your store every day and make a nuisance of themselves. Such people must be told that they are not welcome. If you are firm with them in the beginning, your troubles will be few.

The floor plans illustrated here show some simple, common ways of doing a video store layout.

A TYPICAL STRIP CENTER STORE LAYOUT — 1,100 SQ. FT.

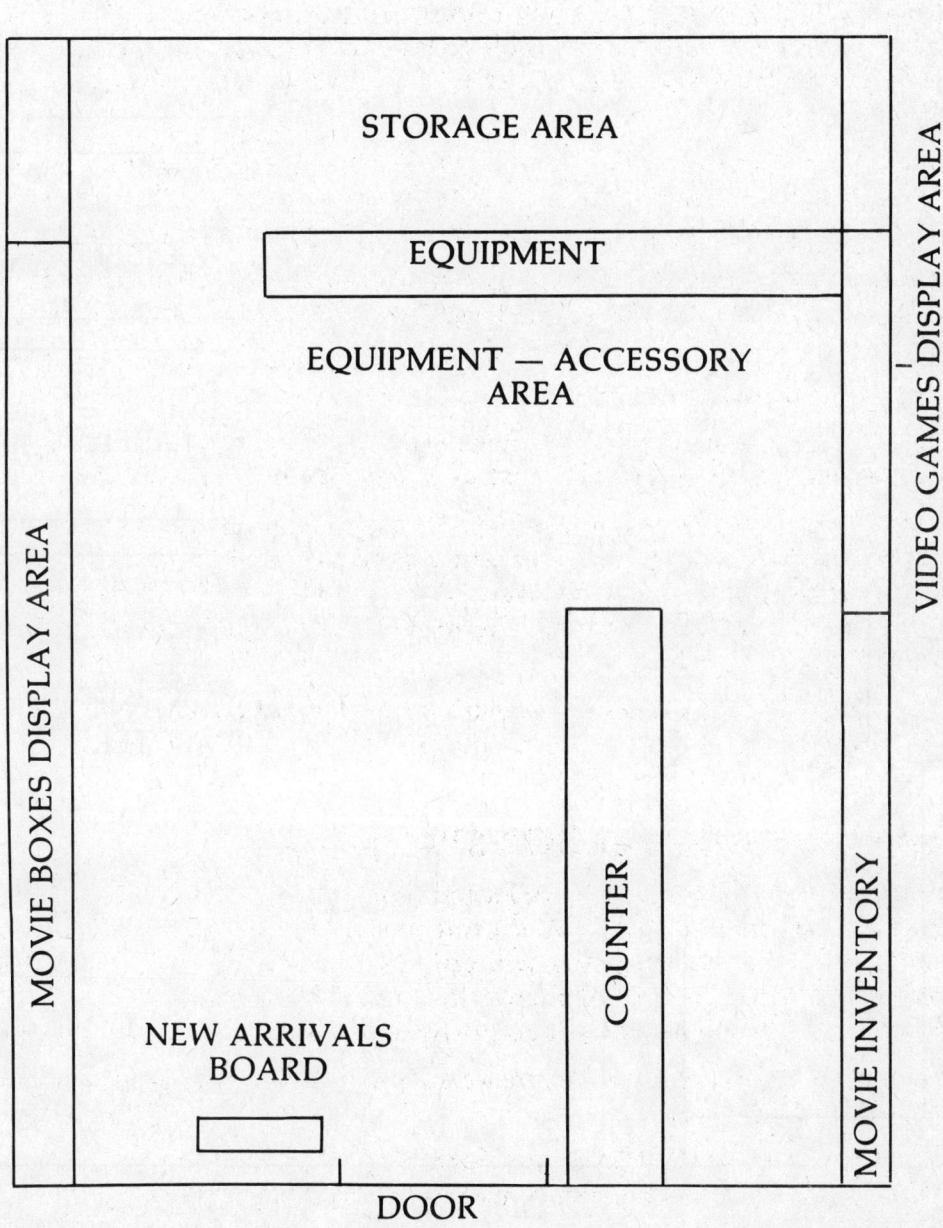

A TYPICAL FREE-STANDING STORE LAYOUT — 1,800 SQ. FT.

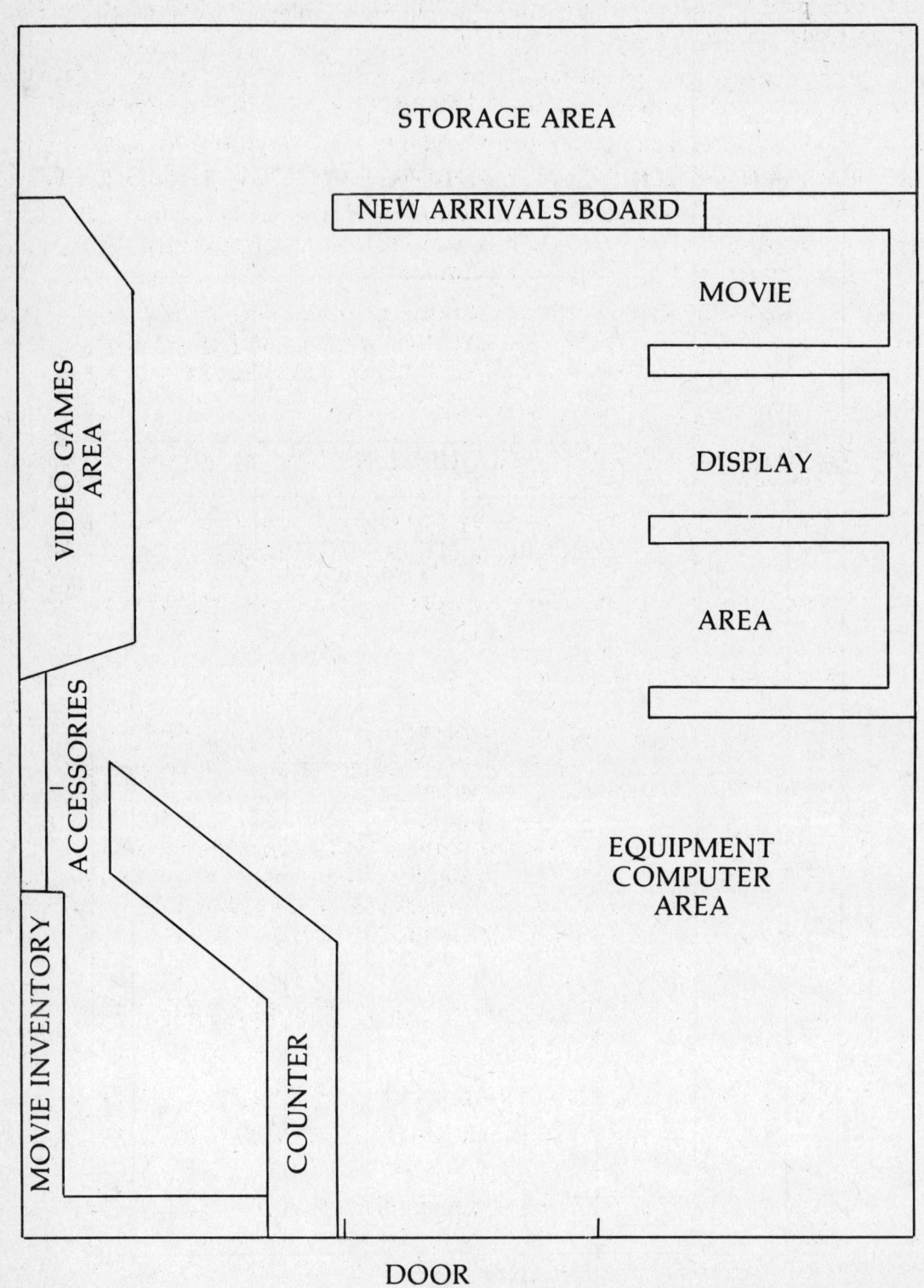

When you lease your store, the rent is usually calculated by the square foot or square meter. You are in fact paying for the area covered by the entire floor space — from the floor to the ceiling.

The astute store owner will try to maximize the use of every foot of space to generate profit. Walls are one of the most neglected spaces in business outlets. You should try to use them efficiently.

In the video business, walls can be used to display movie boxes. Some space can also be used for the display of "plan-o-grams" of video accessories.

Ceilings are the least usable space in your store, but you can hang advertising mobiles from the ceiling. They give a good air of activity and festivity in a store.

Not only must you plan floor space in the selling area, you must plan the area used for storage. Make sure staff do not clutter up the store room and make storage of boxes and products a nightmare.

The people who know square foot profit planning best are the ones who run supermarkets. They know how to mass merchandise and emphasize a product that gives them the best return on investment per square foot.

Here is how they calculate square feet.

(a) Take the lineal footage of a gondola, stand, or wall rack on which a certain kind of product is displayed.

(b) Multiply the lineal footage by the depth of the display base.

(c) Double the figure for the *burden rate* of aisles, checkouts, stock rooms, etc.

(d) Multiply this by the percentage of space actually occupied by the product under review.

The formula looks like this:

$$\text{Length} \times \text{Depth} \times 2 \times \text{percent of product space} = \text{square feet chargeable to product}$$

Next, apply the sales of the product to the square foot chargeable to find out your profit per square foot. For example, assume your sales of accessories equalled $1,700 in November. These accessories are displayed on a rack 3 feet long by 1-1/2 feet deep. This rack takes up 2% of your space.

Using the calculation above:

$$3 \times 1\text{-}1/2 \times 2 \times 2\% = 0.18 \text{ square feet chargeable.}$$

Now multiply your sales by your square feet chargeable:

$$\$1,700 \times 0.18 = \$306 \text{ profit per square foot.}$$

This formula can help you decide what products you should be devoting more space and sales effort to.

In planning your store, always keep in mind that one day you have to grow. You may expand your movie inventory, your rental machine stock, or your accessories. Always bear in mind you must not tear everything down in order to expand. It is not costly, but it is a great disturbance to your customers.

5

YOUR OPERATING BUDGET

All businesses must operate within a budget to be effective. A budget is like your roadmap. You need it to tell you where to go, and how to go. The budget is, in other words, your plan to profits.

First project your sales, first by month, and then by quarter (see Sample #2).

Next, project your quarterly gross profits (see Sample #3).

Once you know what your gross profits are, you can tailor your expenses according to your means. For example, using the figures in Samples #2 and #3, you must not spend more than $347,700 in that year or you will have a loss. In fact, as you will see in Sample #4, the Expense Budget, you should not spend more than $196,150. To achieve a good net profit, you must minimize costs and expenses and maximize sales.

SAMPLE #2
BUDGET

Sales Forecast	1st qtr.	2nd qtr.	3rd qtr.	4th qtr.	Total
Equipment sales	$120,000	$125,000	$119,000	$140,000	$ 504,000
Equipment rentals	40,000	42,000	45,000	50,000	177,000
Movie sales	5,000	6,000	2,000	6,000	19,000
Movie rentals	36,000	40,000	42,000	50,000	168,000
Video games sales	46,000	50,000	52,000	70,000	218,000
Video games rentals	2,000	4,000	4,000	6,000	16,000
Accessories sales	6,000	8,000	8,000	9,000	31,000
Others	1,000	1,000	1,000	1,000	4,000
	$256,000	$276,000	$273,000	$332,000	$1,137,000

SAMPLE #3
ESTIMATED GROSS PROFITS

Profit	1st qtr.	2nd qtr.	3rd qtr.	4th qtr.	Total
Equipment sales (20%)	$24,000	$25,000	$23,800	$ 28,000	$100,800
Equipment rentals (40%)	16,000	16,800	18,000	20,000	70,800
Movie sales (25%)	1,300	1,500	500	1,500	4,800
Movie rentals (55%)	19,800	22,000	23,100	27,500	92,400
Video games sales (25%)	11.500	12,500	13,000	17,500	54,500
Video games rentals (50%)	1,500	2,000	2,000	3,000	8,500
Accessories sales (45%)	2,700	3,600	3,600	4,000	13,900
Others (50%)	500	500	500	500	2,000
	$77,300	$83,900	$84,500	$102,000	$347,700

SAMPLE #4
EXPENSE BUDGET

Expenses	1st qtr.	2nd qtr.	3rd qtr.	4th qtr.	Total
Accounting and legal	$ 100	$ 100	$ 100	$ 200	$ 500
Advertising	3,000	2,000	2,500	4,000	11,500
Bad debts	100	100	100	100	400
Bank charges and interest	800	1,200	1,000	2,000	5,000
Business licenses and taxes	1,500	—	—	—	1,500
Commissions paid	8,000	7,000	7,500	12,000	34,500
Depreciation	4,500	4,000	4,500	5,500	18,500
Employee benefits	200	200	300	350	1,050
Insurance	1,000	1,000	1,000	1,000	4,000
Office expenses	500	500	500	500	2,000
Promotion and entertainment	1,000	1,000	1,000	1,000	4,000
Rent	3,300	3,300	3,300	3,300	13,200
Salaries	22,500	22,500	22,500	24,500	92,000
Telephone	500	500	500	500	2,000
Travel	500	500	500	500	2,000
Utilities	750	750	750	1,750	4,000
	$48,250	$44,650	$46,050	$57,200	$196,150

Projected gross profit = $347,700

Projected total expenses = $196,150

Projected net profit = $151,550

Armed with your projections, you should operate your store under these target figures. At the same time, you should strive to achieve the sales projections using the expenses as the guide.

You must control your budget. You set performance standards for your staff to achieve. Periodically, you should measure the actual results and analyze the difference between actual and planned performance.

Sample #5 illustrates the inter-relationships between those two elements — budgeting and measurement of performance.

SAMPLE #5
BUDGETARY PLANNING AND PERFORMANCE REVIEW PROCESS

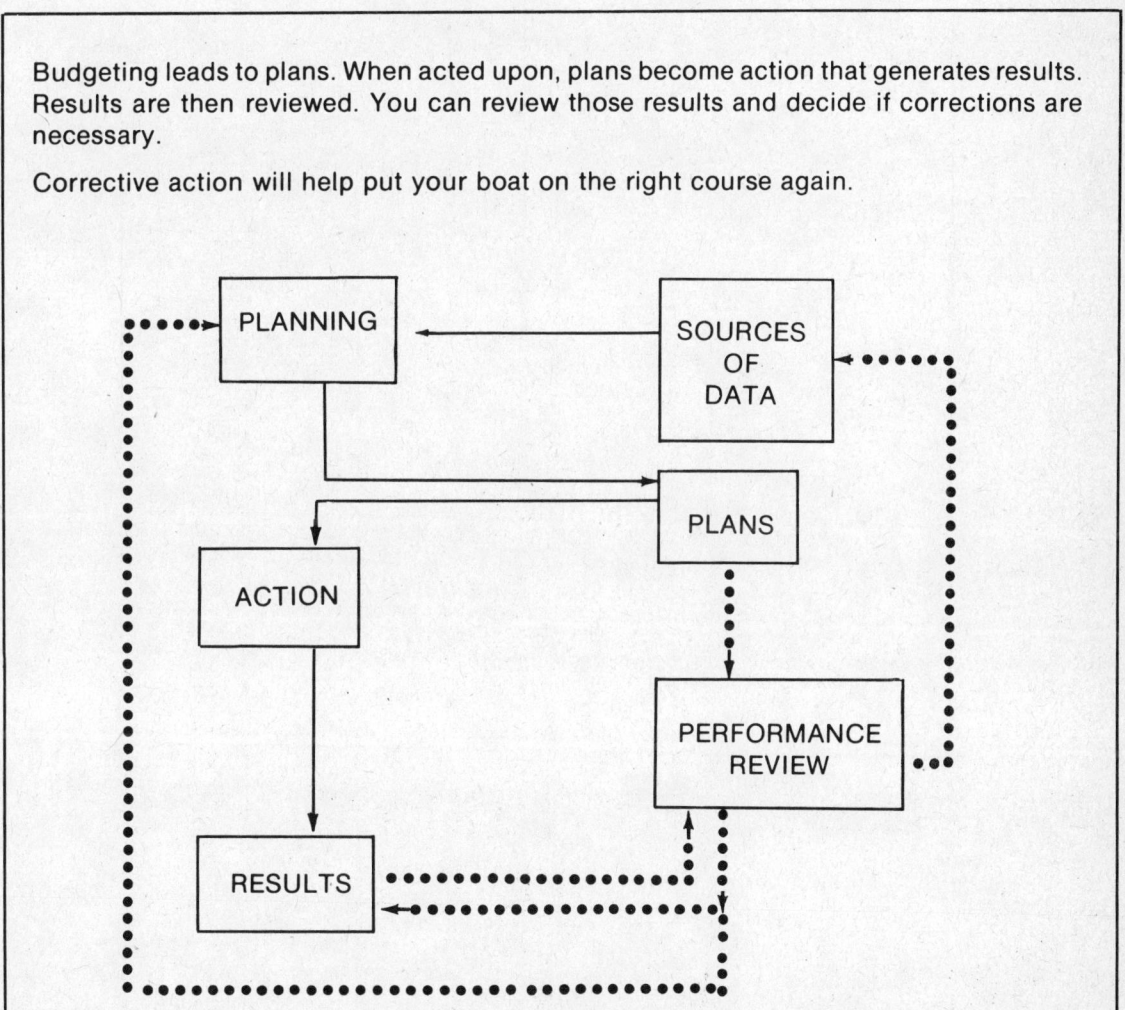

Budgeting leads to plans. When acted upon, plans become action that generates results. Results are then reviewed. You can review those results and decide if corrections are necessary.

Corrective action will help put your boat on the right course again.

In summary, budgeting is an integral part of your business. To some, it is boring work, but if you do not have a budget you do not have a goal. And if you do not have a goal, you do not have a direction for success.

6

WHAT TYPE OF BUSINESS STRUCTURE SHOULD YOU CHOOSE

Businesses can be formed in one of three different ways: proprietorships, partnerships, or corporations. Whichever form you choose for your video retail outlet, be sure to find out the legal process for forming your company in your region. The laws and regulations vary from region to region but the basic structure is the same.

Another choice you have is buying into a franchise operation. Franchises are growing more popular, and they offer an alternative for people who would like guidance and structure from the "head office," but still have some independence.

a. A PROPRIETORSHIP

The simplest form of business organization is a proprietorship, which usually involves one person (or sometimes a husband-wife team). It is the simplest form because, to get started, all you really need is a business license and something to sell.

A sole proprietor is the one who owns the business. The proprietor is the person who has legal title or an exclusive right to the property. In most cases he or she is the one who runs it too.

A sole proprietorship has its advantages and its drawbacks. It means that 100% of the profits go to the owner. But a sole proprietor also suffers if there are losses. He or she is personally liable for all losses.

Also, in a proprietorship, the earnings of your business are your personal earnings. It doesn't matter what form these earnings take (cash, capital equipment, inventory, or accounts receivable). You pay income tax on the business's profits, regardless, at your personal tax rate.

A sole proprietorship usually can react very quickly to market changes. There are no group discussions or committees upon committees to mull over certain problems or projects. The sole owner does *all* the decision making.

b. A PARTNERSHIP

A partnership is an association of two or more persons for the purpose of managing a business. They share in the profits and losses.

Usually each partner has full power to act for the firm in carrying on its business. It makes them proprietors and agents of other co-partners. Not only is each partner individually liable to third persons for the obligations incurred in the business but is equally liable for obligations incurred by co-partners when acting within the scope of the firm's business.

If a partner has paid or been required to pay creditors of the firm from personal assets, other partners may be expected to contribute on an equal basis (or some other agreed upon basis). Partners are subject to unlimited personal liability.

Partnerships have an advantage over sole proprietorships in that losses are not suffered by one person. Also major decisions are made by a group. Input from more than one person can help solve major problems.

Another advantage of a partnership is its capacity to obtain more capital. A sole proprietorship would be limited to the capabilities of one owner.

Unlike corporations, partnerships are treated as groups of persons doing business under a given name, not as a legal person separate and apart from its shareholders. This means that partnerships will be taxed only as personal earnings of the partners.

Partnerships can also be dissolved at any time. When a partner withdraws from the business by choice or by death, the partnership is ended.

c. CORPORATIONS

The process of incorporation differs from region to region. By incorporating, transferable shares are set up for each partner so that in case of death or similar circumstances, dissolution may be avoided.

One of the biggest advantages of setting up a corporation is its limited liability. The loss that a partner or owner may incur is limited to the amount of capital personally invested in the business. Liability does not extend to personal belongings.

I recommend you incorporate your company as soon as possible. Not only do you obtain limited liability by doing so, you have the advantage of several tax benefits. Your accountant will be able to tell you what these tax benefits are in your region.

One disadvantage of a corporation is that, in case it is necessary, dissolving the company is more difficult. You will need legal and accounting advice before you can close a corporation.

Because you have a few partners in your corporation, each partner carries some credit backing. The credit rating of each partner is very valuable to the corporation. When the need arises for more funding, it is possible for all of you to approach your bank for more operating capital. In a case like this your banker would require some security. Usually partners will have to personally guarantee the repayment of the loan. What this means is if you wanted, say $100,000, each partner could pledge personal assets for the return of the loan when it is necessary. Your banker will require each partner to complete a personal statement of his or her net worth. Based on the strength of the statements of net worth the request of the loan will be approved.

d. FRANCHISE OPERATIONS

The principle of franchising is very elementary. Someone has an idea — in this case a design for the "perfect" video store — packages it, and makes money out of selling the package. Instead of owning all the outlets, the franchisor simply sells the rights to use the idea and the name. Usually, the stores will also all use the same furniture, color schemes, and design.

Franchisors usually advertise in the business pages of major newspapers. They also advertise in the business opportunities section of the newspapers.

When buying a franchise you must be very careful. Here are some guidelines to help you.

(a) Study the franchisor's operation. When you walk through the door, study the surroundings. Are the staff busy? They should be if it is a successful franchise. Is the place neat and orderly? If it is, they are organized.

(b) Check out claims of the franchisor. If the franchisor claims that they have 25 stores, find out if the figure is, in fact, correct. If they claim they have the most stores in North America, ask for proof. Do not believe everything they say.

(c) Talk to at least three franchisees. By talking to these people you will gain a wealth of knowledge about the franchisor. Dissatisfied franchisees will tell you all their problems with the franchisor. On the other hand, happy franchisees will be full of praise.

(d) Talk to ex-franchisees. Find out why they aren't still in business. Usually such people will give you a volume of information. But measure all the facts. There are always two sides of the story.

(e) Weigh the package offered. Find out specifically what you get back for the money they want. If the franchise fee is $30,000, find out what you get for it. Do you get cash registers, fixtures, signs, stationery, stock, equipment, etc.? If so, how much do you price each item. Subtract that total from the $30,000 and you will discover what the rest is for the use of the name and goodwill.

(f) Compare all benefits and prices with the other franchisors you have met. To make a good decision, make yourself a table of comparisons.

(g) All franchise stores purchased can also be sold. Each franchisor has rules and conditions regarding resale of a franchise. Usually it depends on the qualifications of the prospective buyer. The franchisor has the final say about whether the prospective buyer will be approved, which is fair because it is the franchisor who has to get along with the buyer, not you.

However, your franchise store has a residual value. You should make a good estimate of what you think the store is worth in five years time. Include the figure in your decision-making process.

For detailed information about buying a franchise, see the book *Franchising* by Michael M. Coltman, Self-Counsel Press.

7
HIRING YOUR PERSONNEL

Personnel management experts have written volumes about this subject. Interviewing and hiring is an art. For some of you, it may be the first time you are sitting on the hiring side of the table. This section ought to help you.

a. FINDING GOOD STAFF

Everyone knows the importance of hiring the right people. Your staff is a reflection of your entire operation. Most supervisors spend 50 to 70% of their time coaching, training, and trying to motivate people in their organization. Therefore, hiring good people at the start will make your job easier.

Most business people learn early that it is impossible to appraise applicants by their appearance and personality alone. Some charming personalities with glib tongues turn out to be good people and others are poor employees.

The resume and the application form are the source of background information on the candidate. Their purpose is to help you screen out the unsuitable candidate and provide information on the candidate's education, past training, and job experience.

The way an application form and resume is presented tells a great deal. It shows how much the applicant is interested in the job. If a great amount of work is put into typing or handwriting out the resume, you know that the person is at least very interested in acquiring a job.

The application form can be used to screen out potential employees. Whenever people present themselves at your office or store, ask them to complete the application form. Tell them that you will want to review it immediately. This gives you a chance to talk to them and assure that no time is wasted in case the education, experience, and training needed are not met.

The more information you can collect about the applicant's history, the better you can gauge the person. Armed with this information, you can generally predict the applicant's future performance.

The application form is the most important document the applicant will provide. You can have one printed up to resemble the example in Sample #6.

SAMPLE #6
APPLICATION FORM

APPLICATION FORM

Your Company Name
Address
Phone Number

Name _____

Address _____

_____

Postal / Zip Code _____

Telephone Number _____

Employment History

1. Company _____

Address _____

Telephone Number _____

Supervisor _____

Duties and Responsibilities _____

_____

Reason for Leaving _____

Employed from _____ to _____

2. Company _____

Address _____

Telephone Number _____

Supervisor _____

Duties and Responsibilities _____

_____

Reason for Leaving _____

Employed from _____ to _____

Education History

	School	Course	From	To	Level Attained
High School					
College					
University					
Part time or Continuing Education					

How did you generally do in school? _____

_____

Describe extra-curricular activities you were involved in _____

_____

List any official positions held _____

_____

List any achievements in these activities _____

_____

What are your hobbies? _____

References

	Name	Address	Telephone Number
1.			
2.			
3.			

May we contact them now? _____

I, the undersigned, declare that the above is true to the best of my knowledge.

_____   _____
Date   Applicant's Signature

b. THE JOB DESCRIPTION

Before you begin to hire staff you should draw up a short job description questionnaire for yourself. Fill it out so you know what the job is, what has to be done, and who you should be looking for. (See Sample #7.)

SAMPLE #7
JOB DESCRIPTION QUESTIONNAIRE

```
Position _____  Department _____
Salary range _____
Job description _____
_____
_____
_____
Personal characteristics needed (describe experience and special qualities needed)
_____
_____
_____
Other comments _____
_____
_____
```

One danger a job description sheet can create is it may give birth to a stereotype operation. In a small business, like the video business, the staff you hire ought to do a variety of jobs — from selling to bookkeeping to housekeeping.

Most business managers will insert a clause at the end of each job description sheet that reads: " . . . and whatever else assigned by your supervisor and manager." This clause will erase the danger of too much compartmentalization in your organization. In other words, the person who works at the movie club area can sit in for the person who runs the video recorder rentals, and so on.

c. SCREENING AND INTERVIEWING

During the first or screening interview additional facts about the applicant must be gathered quickly. Use the interview guide on the next page. You will not have time to write down notes while interviewing, but do so as soon as it is over.

Work background
- Tell me more about your work.
- Do you like your work?
- Why do you want to leave your present job?
- What is the longest time you have ever worked at one job?
- Which one did you like best? Why?
- Which did you like least? Why?
- What compliments have you received about your work?
- What criticisms have you been given regarding your previous jobs?

Education background

- Did you like going to school?
- What was your favorite subject?
- What was your least favorite subject?
- During school did you hold office in any extramural activities?
- Did you work part-time during your school days?
- How did you fare in school? Were you top of the class or in between or bottom half?

Social and hobby background
- What are your hobbies?
- Are you active in work-related clubs and other organizations?

Health background
- What have you achieved in your hobby pursuits?
- Can you life heavy objects? (if applicable)

Philosophy and ambitions
- What are you aiming for ultimately?
- What do you see yourself doing five years from now?
- What do you consider are your strongest qualities?

- What are your weakest points?
- What attracts you to this position?

After the interview, make notes about each category, and give the applicant an overall "grade" of fair, good, or excellent.

Shortlisted candidates should be further interviewed. After the interview, you will be able to cut the shortlist to two or three people.

At this point you should call references and inquire about your prospective employee.

Here are some questions you may want to ask:
- When was the candidate employed with you?
- What did the candidate do?
- Was the candidate a good worker?
- Was the candidate honest?
- Did the candidate need much supervision?
- How many staff did the candidate supervise?
- Did the candidate get along with peers?
- What was the candidate's absentee record?
- What were the candidate's strengths?
- What were the candidate's weaknesses?
- Why did he or she leave your employ?
- Would you rehire him or her? Why?
- Overall how would you rate him or her?

d. JOB SCHEDULES

A timetable is a must in retailing. These should be made out every week giving staff two weeks notice on any change in job schedules.

The timetable should be posted in a prominent place like a staff bulletin board.

Make sure the people who are opening the store report earlier so that the carpets are vacuumed and windows cleaned. And ensure that your store is opened every day at the right time, not earlier or later.

Staff who cannot report to work must make alternative arrangements to have the void filled. You should have full knowledge of what is going on or otherwise things will get out of hand.

8
STOCKING YOUR STORE

Buyers for department stores or for any other company will tell you that half the battle of making a good profit for the business is buying right. If you are confident in the buying role, knowing full well you can buy right, you are well on your way to making a good profit for your business. When buying, you must bear in mind the following:

(a) Pricing — are you buying at the best price?

(b) Volume — are you buying the right quantity?

(c) Timing — is this the right time to purchase the product?

(d) Product — is this the right product to purchase?

(e) Selection — what extent of selection is needed to stay competitive?

(f) Competition — what is the competition buying?

(g) Turnover — how fast can I turn over stock?

All these should be in your mind when you make any purchase. The more you study before making a decision, the less chance you have of making a mistake.

Think right and buy right, and you will be well on your way to profit.

a. SELECTING A DISTRIBUTOR

If you read the current magazines on the video and the electronics business, you will see advertisements placed by distributors of all kinds ranging from hardware or equipment to software and accessories. There are big distributors who have branches dotted all over the continent. They stock a wide range of products and have very efficient distribution systems. There are the medium size distributors that are striving and trying hard to establish a bigger foothold in the industry. And there are the smaller ones that are hungry, who try hard and who probably deserve some support.

Some of the better known distributors have sales offices in every major city in North America, or they have manufacturer's representatives whose income depends on the commissions earned through selling for other distributors. Most video magazines usually publish an annual directory of those involved in the video business.

Major cities will also have information in the yellow pages on video wholesalers and suppliers. If you cannot find a category like that, turn to the stereophonic section. There will be some listings there. Other video operators might be able to give you some leads, too.

After you have obtained a few names and addresses, call the distributors' offices and make an appointment. Video distributors are very busy because of the boom, so call ahead.

The more professional you are in your approach toward your potential distributor, the more you will get — if not in price at least in attention, service, and favors.

Before you make a decision about a distributor, you should ask a lot of questions about the operation. Check out what kind of stock is usually around on a normal working day. Listen to their sales pitch and then ask your questions. Make sure you cover the following ground:

(a) What are the pricing structures and policies?

(b) Does the distributor have all the major lines of movies?

(c) What other dealers use this distributor? When you find out who else uses a particular distributor, you can ask those dealers if they have had any problems.

(d) Do they have a workable backorder system?

(e) Are they a one-stop shop?

After you have interviewed a few distributors, you will have a good idea about which one can provide you with the best service.

b. TAKE ADVANTAGE OF SALES TERMS

All sales distributors have different sales policies. As a customer you should study all the terms and conditions so that you are fully aware of the grounds you are dealing with.

The attractiveness of the terms offered depends on how hungry or how aggressive the distributor is. Some distributors will not extend any credit to newcomers to the trade. These distributors will only want to deal with you on a cash on delivery basis. Usually these are suppliers of popular products. They can afford to do this because they know that you will want their products enough to pay cash.

If you can afford to pay cash for products, do so. Not only will you usually get a fair cash discount, but you will know exactly where you are in financial terms. In other words, if you do not have the money, you should not be buying.

There are other distributors who can afford or are forced to extend credit to qualified customers. Most credit applications are thoroughly checked out. Your bank will be contacted, as will your references. These distributors are taking a risk by selling you a product on credit.

1. Net 30 days

Net 30 days means that you can buy products from a distributor and you are given 30 days to pay for the product. During prosperous times 30 days can drag on to 45 or 60 days.

Suppose you purchase a movie on October 5. Most dealers will wait for the statement of accounts, which they will not receive until after October has gone by — usually in early or mid-November. If you pay the outstanding amount by the end of November the distributor will not quibble.

In reality, you received terms of 55 days. Taking advantage of sales terms like that means that you have about 55 days to rent that movie free of cost. If the movie cost about $60, you would have made a tidy profit.

2. 5%, 30 days, net 31 days

This term means you can buy products at the usual 30 days, but when you pay, you are allowed to deduct 5% off the invoice. These are very attractive terms. When you are invoiced, you should not forget to pay the net amount or you will be penalized the 5%.

If you consistently buy a great volume from the dealer you will find these terms are a little cumbersome. You will have to keep a watchful eye on the accounts so that you do not let the rebate slip by. But the 5% is worth it. If your volume is substantial, try negotiating with your distributor and come to an agreement where you can pay your invoices once or twice a month less the 5% discount.

Some distributors will even go as far as giving 10%, 30 day terms. You can be sure that these distributors have built a good proportion of that 10% into the price. But if you buy from them, you would be foolish not to take advantage of the discounts.

3. 2%, 10 days, net 30 days

This means you have 30 days to pay for the purchases. However, if you have the money and you pay by 10 days of the invoice, you are allowed to take 2% off the invoice total.

If interest rates are hovering around the 10% rate, these terms are attractive. However, if the bank rates are high, such terms are not very attractive.

4. 2%, 10th following month

If you bought a product on November 1, under these terms, you would not have to pay before December 10. And if you did, you could take off 2% from the invoice. Otherwise you pay at the end of the following month.

5. Dating

During buying shows some distributors will offer attractive dating terms to dealers. Dating privileges usually come during the fall buying periods for video stores. By dating, dealers are usually told that they have a longer period to pay for products. Dating may appear in the form of paying half by 30 days, a quarter by 60, and the rest by 90 days. These terms are excellent if you can control your cash flow and make certain that at the end of each dated period you dutifully pay what was agreed upon between you and your supplier.

The danger in dating is that you can get carried away and overbuy. Some dealers tend to buy the fringe items as well and some distributors will insist that you buy prepacks when dating is allowed. These items can be very difficult to sell.

6. Shipping terms

Shipping terms vary from distributor to distributor. Some will pay for shipping no matter what or how many items are purchased. In a case like this you must suspect that the cost of shipping has been built into the price, or that the items sold have a very long margin.

Some distributors will prepay shipping if purchases exceed a given dollar volume. In such cases, back orders are usually sent out prepaid as well.

Other distributors will send out shipments prepaid but charged in the invoice. This method eliminates the need to pay the shipping company every time a shipment comes in.

c. FLOOR PLAN PURCHASES

Floor plans or floor planning is a rather common term in the television and appliance industries. Now with video hitting the entertainment and leisure scene, floor planning will become just as important to video stores.

Floor planning is a financial arrangement between a manufacturer, a finance company, and a retailer. These three parties devise a scheme that allows a retailer to receive substantial inventory and delay payment until the product is sold. Usually, if the product is unsold over a period of time, probably 90 days, the dealer is obligated to pay the finance company interest, usually at 1.5 to 3% per month (30% per annum).

Floor plans benefit manufacturers because the finance company pays the invoice at a discount within a short period of time after shipping the product to the retailer. By participating in the floor plan scheme, most dealers tend to buy more because of the advantage of not having to put out money immediately.

There are many variations of floor plans. Interest rates, interest free periods, and credit lines vary from one dealer to another, and from one manufacturer to the other. However, in all cases, floor plans help cash poor dealers to carry inventory, freeing capital for other purposes such as promotions, expansion, or operating expenses.

If you are a participant of floor plans, you will require a system of tight inventory control. The best system involves diligent attention to accounts payable. You must pay the finance company as soon as the equipment is sold. This method will eliminate the possibility of forgetting to pay your floor plan payments.

The finance companies will always have a representative call on you once a month to audit your floor plan stock if they suspect you are delaying payments. The representative will check serial numbers and match them with the invoices. If a serial number cannot be found in the store the equipment is considered sold and payment will be demanded.

The best solution to the floor planning problem is to run a register of what units are under floor plan. As soon as a piece of equipment is sold, make a notation that it is sold and take down the serial number. Make sure your register is updated when each sale is made. At the end of each week, total the sale, add up the cost of the equipment, and send the finance company the appropriate amount.

Floor planning has spread into the video field rather quickly. As a video retailer, you can approach finance companies like Borg Warner Acceptance, Finance America, Westinghouse Credit Corporation, or ITT Diversified Credit Corporation for more information regarding their policies. If you are attending any major electronic or video shows in the near future, stop at their booths and ask them questions.

The main thing you have to remember about floor planning is that the sooner you sell the equipment on floor plan, the better for your store. And the sooner you pay for the equipment, the fewer headaches you will have. If you neglect to pay on time interest charges will apply, and generally they are pretty stiff.

9

YOUR CHOICE OF STOCK

a. HARDWARE

What equipment should you stock in your store? That will depend mainly on your available capital. If you have a lot of money, you can look into many different lines. You may even carry different brands of one line. But if you have limited capital, I suggest you shop wisely and carry only very popular name brands.

One line you cannot ignore is video cassette recorders whether they be VHS or Beta. In this category there are many brands that will be good sellers. Check your video magazines and you will see full-color advertising by these manufacturers.

In the 1982 Video Retailers Survey conducted by *The Video Store*, retailers were asked to name the best selling brands in six different hardware categories. The following are the results of that survey:

VCRs	VIDEO CAMERAS	PROJECTION TVs
1. RCA	RCA	Sony
2. Panasonic	Panasonic	RCA
3. Sony	Sony	Mitsubishi

VIDEO GAME CONSOLES*	VIDEO DISK PLAYERS	STANDARD TVs
1. Atari	RCA	Sony
2. Mattel	Pioneer	RCA
3. Odyssey 2	Magnavox	Zenith

When selecting your hardware lines, you will learn that manufacturers and distributors often have some form of territorial protection for their existing dealers. A Hitachi sales representative, for example, will not foolishly take your order if he already has a dealer within a couple of miles who is doing a good job. If

---

*This is a rather fluid business. By mid-1983, ColecoVision was the best seller. The other lines disappeared from the market.

you are in a situation like this, it is best to approach other brand name distributors. But do not forget to approach the best selling brand first. You will never know, sometimes even if there is an existing dealer in your trading area, you may be given the line.

b. ACCESSORIES

A video store cannot ignore accessories. Not only are the profit margins better than for equipment, they are very easy to sell.

There are all kinds of accessories available from a host of manufacturers and packaging companies. They range from coaxial cables (bulk or packaged) to splitters to videophile gold ends to stabilizers and enhancers, etc.

Among the more popular accessories are headcleaners. There are many available brands that sell very well. Select those that are wet and dry cleaners — as they are the best. And for cleaning fluid, select those that have freon-bases because the fluid will dry faster than alcohol-based fluids. Note that the new generation of front load Betamax recorders may have problems with automatic headcleaners. The cleaners get easily jammed in those machines. In such recorders, I recommend a manual cleaning using a good cleaning solution and clean chamois sticks or swabs.

Do not ignore stabilizers and enhancers. They sell well too, because they correct rolling and skewing in images.

Another good accessory to carry is stereo sound simulators. These have become very popular because of the poor quality speakers and inefficient amplifiers installed in television sets. You can hook up a stereo sound simulator from the video set of a VCR directly to a set of good speakers. Another way of doing it is through the earphone outlet to your stereo amplifier which in turn will give you effective sound through your home speakers.

Things like adaptors, switchers, coaxial cables, and other odds and ends all add up to your sales. They may not look like much when you ring up a $2 sale each time, but they will make a difference in the end.

The best way of merchandising such small accessories is by ordering a display board sold by packaging companies. But a warning: do not buy a "prepack." All prepacks have several slow movers. Pick and choose good selling items, and get the distributor to help you make your own prepack. Also ask for an exchange policy for any items that never move.

c. VHS versus BETA

The Video Home System (VHS), a half-inch format, has the most followers, not because it is a better system, but because more manufacturers produce VCRs in this format. The parent company, that is, the company that holds the licensing rights, is Matsushita Electric Industrial Company Ltd. It has licensed many other electronic giants to produce their own VCRs including the string of its own subsidiaries and affiliates.

Among the better known brands available in the VHS format are: Akai, JVC, Curtis Mathes, RCA, Mitsubishi (or MGA in the United States), Hitachi, Sharp, Quasar, Magnavox (or Philips), Panasonic, Technics, Sylvania, General Electric, Fisher and so on. Quite an array of brands! Add to those names house brands like J.C. Penny and Montgomery Ward, two very large department store chains in the United States.

On the other front there is the Betamax format, a system that is giving the VHS a good run for the money. Even though it is available under fewer brand names, its presence in the market is very prominent. The Sony Corporation, the inventor of the format, has great hopes for it. Piles of money and effort have been devoted to the promotion and sale of the Betamax machine. Likewise Sanyo, another Japanese electronic giant, has poured millions of dollars into promoting and advertising the format.

You now have to decide on the selection of movie formats and equipment for your inventory. Let us examine the difference in systems without going into the technicalities, which should be left to technical people. Decision makers only need to know what they are and not how they are made.

1. The differences

VHS uses a video cassette that is larger in size than the Betamax cassette. Yet the width of the tapes are both half-inch. Both cassettes do the same job; they are inserted into the tape recorder for recording and playback.

The VHS system is the slower of the two formats. The faster the tape travels past the recording head, the better the recording. More tape is utilized too! Therefore, the Betamax, because it is faster, is a better quality reproduction format.

However, the difference in quality reproduction between the two systems is not great. When monitored through today's television sets, the layperson cannot easily tell the difference. However, if you view the same program through a good component television set, you will see a difference.

If there is no marked difference in quality, what will the consumer demand be? That is the question that a video retailer would naturally ask. It is an important topic. You would like to know where to spend your inventory budget.

2. Making your choice

In order to determine that answer you must do some leg work. Call on electronic and video stores in the area you propose to set up your business. Ask questions about the two systems and find out which format they sell more of.

During your rounds scout your competition. Ask questions like a consumer would. The more you learn about your competitor the better.

Or, go into the store, introduce yourself and ask pertinent questions. A good number will probably help you out. I know of a few cases where friendships have developed and they subsequently formed their own buying groups.

Before making up your mind on the format selection also talk to your suppliers and a movie distributor. They usually can read market trends. They can tell you whether their Beta sales are increasing by significant percentages or not.

Talk to equipment sales representatives. Naturally a Quasar sales representative will say VHS is better, and a Sanyo representative will favor Beta. You will have to read in between the lines. Most representatives have a wealth of knowledge about the video business. Their daily contact with video stores will be your gain.

3. Market trends

At the time of writing, VHS was outselling Beta. In the video survey mentioned above, it was discovered that of all VCR units sold in 1982, 72% were VHS and 28% were Beta.

There is now some indication that the gap is closing steadily as prices become lower in the Beta format.

Some video operators have decided to play it safe. They keep both formats in movies and stock both formats in equipment. These stores naturally have a larger inventory, and more capital tied down.

If you don't have the funds to stock every movie in both formats, you might just stock what I call *top-con* titles in both Beta and VHS formats. Top-con titles are those 100 or so titles that you are convinced are a must.

If your budget is good enough to stock every title in both formats, you will not have the problem of a decision on which one to select. On the other hand, if you do not have enough money to spend, you should stay away from catalogue titles in both formats, or get just one. For example, you may buy just one format (probably a VHS) of, say, *Pride and Prejudice*, not because it is not a good movie, but because it is not a very popular item in a movie club.

I have compiled a list of top-con movie titles on page 97. These are the top 200 titles of 1982-83. It will, of course, change from time to time.

One other trend you should watch is the price of hardware. Often, manufacturers are able to cut costs or are forced to lower their profit margins by competition. As a result lower prices are available. For example, Betamax machine prices dropped $500 in one year.

What does this mean? It means that these machines are now within the reach of a lot more pockets. Frequently, department stores cash in on such opportunities and buy big volume. Volume buying can enable a store to offer fantastic prices on machines. More machines sold means more customers for a movie club. It follows that if Beta manufacturers are lowering their prices, you will be getting more Beta consumers.

Below is a comparison of the two formats based on 1982 sales.*

	VHS	BETA
Price of movies	same	same
Percentage of consumers	72%	28%
Potential	good	good
Numbers of manufactures of machines	more	less
Numbers of movies available	same	same
Quality of reproduction	good	better
Advertising	excellent	excellent

On software, 70% of dealers chose VHS. The table below shows a profile of retailers choice of pre-recorded inventory by format.

	1982	1981
VHS and Beta Combination	54%	41%
VHS only	18%	17%
Beta only	4%	2%

d. THE DISK FORMATS

While the tape cassette formats are very important to the video business, the disk formats shouldn't be overlooked. They are in the video market to stay. At the time of writing, sales of the disk machines are still struggling to make a significant mark in the video market. By numbers they lag far behind VCRs. In fact, according to *Money Magazine*, RCA was a real loser in 1981 because they only made 30% of their forecast in the sale of disk players. However, in the sale of video disks the reverse was true. For every machine RCA sold, they expected to sell about 7 disks. When results were tabulated, RCA found that they sold 30 disks per machine. The remarkable find was that consumers were buying disks. This was not surprising because there were very few places where one could rent movie disks.

---

*The Video Store, September, 1982.

Lately, Twentieth Century Fox also began producing more video disks for the market. This is encouraging news. As well, another company, Vestron, has introduced some titles. There are more and more companies selling disks which will help the disk cause. If more software becomes available, more machines will be sold.

The good thing about the video disk market is the price of both hardware and software. One could buy a player for about $200 in the U.S. or about $400 in Canada. A video disk could be purchased for about $30 in the United States. These lower prices mean that more people could begin buying disks as a collection.

At present, two disk systems are in the forefront of the market. They are the Capacitance Electronic Disk (CED) and the Laser Disk system. There is another system that has been shown in electronic shows, but has not yet hit the market. This is the VHD or Video High Density system.

If you want to go into the video disk rental business, the natural choice is the CED system. Not only are there more machines on the market, there are also more disks available. Although the laser disk system is more sophisticated, and the quality of the reproduction better, there are fewer laser systems in the video consumers homes.

e. HOW MANY TO BUY?

Estimating how many pieces to buy is always difficult. I cannot teach you this aspect of the game. It comes to you with experience. Don't be afraid to make mistakes; you will learn from them. The important thing is that you must not repeat the same mistakes. Buy according to market trends.

For example, suppose you are planning to promote a basic model of VCR in the month of October. You must bear in mind that:

(a) The schools have already started for a new year, which can cause a temporary lull in sales.

(b) Christmas is just around the corner and there will be people who will be doing early shopping.

(c) New fall television programming in North America begins and there will be people who will want to record new fall programs.

Bearing these points in mind you can make up your estimates. Consult your sales people at a meeting and get a commitment from the group for the success of the campaign.

Use this approach with every large purchase decision or promotional campaign.

f. CHOOSING GOOD MOVIES

In running a video store, the selection of the right movies for the right clientele is very important. Surveys have found that *all* people like feature films. Of those, 51% were age 30 to 34. Customers between the ages of 18 and 24 prefer to watch concerts more than any other age group. The survey also found that four times as many singles as married couples rent adult films.

As a video store owner, you will have to find out what your customers like to see in your stock. Many stores have a running "want" list. Customers are asked "What do you like to watch most? — by title." Also keep a running list of the movies customers ask for.

Following are a few tips on how to buy the right movies. Also see Appendix 1 for the top 200 movies in 1983.

- (a) Don't use your own taste as a guide. Do not go by what you think is a good movie. Go by what your customers think is a good movie.

- (b) Buy "top-con" films. Feature films are top-con products no matter what kind of reviews they receive. For example, the movie *Annie* received bad reviews, but in video *Annie* did very well. It was a general movie that anyone could watch at home.

- (c) Buy movies that won awards. They all rent well because of the good publicity.

- (d) If the local disc jockey has recommended a certain movie as a must to see, get that movie. Chances are 10,000 listeners have heard the recommendation.

- (e) Do not ignore movies that have a bad reputation. For example, *The Attack of the Killer Tomatoes* was reputed to be the worst movie ever made. Yet dealers claim that the cassette is a winner. Based on its bad reputation alone, customers are curious enough to spend a few dollars to find out why it was the worst movie ever made.

- (f) All horror movies — if the quality is reasonably good — are good movers. Kids will watch them over and over, and adults like them too.

- (g) Children's movies move very well. Walt Disney movies are very strong.

- (h) Black and white movies do not rent very well unless they are well-known classics.

Once you have chosen a movie, you have to decide how many copies to buy. Depth stocking is the term used for buying multiple copies. You should have doubles of movies that are sure hits, but be more cautious with borderline movies. It's not always a problem to have a movie unavailable as you can suggest other movies to rent while the customer waits for the most popular one to be available.

Caution: After you buy a movie, remove the tabs that are at the back of the prerecorded cassette. This ensures that the movie will not be recorded over by careless customers.

g. THE MOVIE REGISTER

One of the most important and useful documents in your purchasing operation is the movie register. Basically it is a list of movies you have purchased over the years. All you need is a book that has alphabetical tabs. As you buy movies, list every purchase alphabetically in the book. Include in your entries such information as cost, format, date of purchase, and where you bought it.

Below is an example of what a typical page in a movie register looks like.

TITLE	COST	VHS	BETA	BOUGHT FROM	DATE

The register will tell you at a glance what movies you have in your store. If you have more than 200 titles, you will not be able to remember all of them. When you are at a distributor, you can use the book to check what format of a title you have, which titles you are missing, and which titles you need duplicates of.

The register can tell you at a quick glance how much you paid for a movie. You can then compare distributors' costs.

The movie register can also tell your insurance company how much a stolen movie cost. Insurance companies may want to see actual invoices, but most adjusters will accept your register.

Lastly, if you sell your store at a later date, this record will be very useful when calculating your assets in movies.

h. ORGANIZATIONS THAT CAN HELP

1. AVA

AVA, the American Video Association, was formed to give the independent dealer buying clout with video manufacturers. AVA claims to have about 450 dealer members across North America. As such they are assured the best prices in all kinds of video products. They also have a video movie exchange that may be helpful to those dealers who need to pad their library.

AVA can be reached at 2634 W. Baseline Road, Mesa, Arizona 85202, (602) 838-7157 or (800) 528-7400.

2. VSDA

VSDA, the Video Software Dealers Association, is a non-profit association of video retailers. Formed in January, 1982, VSDA has been the political voice for the video business. Members of the organization include distributors of prerecorded cassettes who must be happy to see the association side with them against piracy.

Benefits derived from joining an organization such as VSDA are many. There is invaluable information in their newsletters. A member can also participate in their popular bankcard program which enables the smaller retailer to qualify for a 2.5% credit card merchant processing rate versus the regular 4 to 5% paid by most retailers. Members of VSDA can also participate in their store bag program which entitles dealers to purchase store bags at a reduced rate.

VSDA can be reached at 10087 Astoria Boulevard, Cherry Hill, New Jersey 08034, (609) 424-7404.

10

THE NEW AGE AND VIDEO RETAILING

a. VIDEO GAMES

Video games are not a passing fad. In 1979 400,000 units were sold. Estimates for 1983 are that 7.2 million units will be sold. Sale of game cartridges rose from 4 million units to 70 million between 1979 and 1983. These high figures should convince you to consider video games as part of your new business.

In 1982 there were only three video game systems on the market. In just one year the number of manufacturers grew to eight. These games have widened the choices available to the millions of people who have discovered this new and exciting way to have fun with their television set.

At the same time, game cartridges, a copy of the arcade type video games, were introduced into the market. The game cartridges sold like hot cakes. Today there are hundreds of cartridges on sale in electronic games alone.

The biggest number of game systems sold today are by ColecoVision followed by Atari VCS and then Vectrex. Each one of them is an independent product system. In other words, you cannot use a Vectrex cartridge on an Atari VCS console. However, ColecoVision, which was introduced in mid-1982, has a console that accepts both Atari VCS and Mattel Intellivision cartridges. This makes the system very desirable.

As a store owner, I would advise you to shop carefully for your game lines. The business is a cut-throat one. Mass merchandisers are in the business in a very big way. During peak buying periods, these operations will use the games as loss leaders (or make a minute profit) to draw crowds to their store and hence to their other departments.

Don't slash your prices even though your competitor has. Check around and find out what stock your competitor has. If, for example, your competitor has only 20 or 30 sets left in stock, around peak selling periods (October to December) you will find that even your distributors will be short of supply. If that is the case, lay low until your competitor has exhausted stock, then sell your games at full list price if you wish!

Make your profit when you can. Timing is important.

1. Video game rentals

One way of improving your profit margin is to rent your video game consoles. This part of the business works well. Use the same system as you would on VCR rentals. Assume your Atari VCS costs you $150. Your cartridges cost you, say, $25. If you rented the machine plus two cartridges for $10 a day, in 20 days they would have paid for themselves.

2. Video game consumers

Video games have been estimated to have reached only 5% of North American homes. This product has the tremendous potential of reaching at least twice that many by 1984. That increase would immediately create a flood of demand for game cartridges. But you need to know who your consumers will be to effectively market the product.

The video game consumer has changed in recent years. Here are four basic categories of video game consumers.

(a) The first are the cautious ones. They look for low end unit for standard game play.

(b) The second type wants a game console that gives the satisfaction of a real arcade game. Nowadays some satisfaction is possible due to improvements in cartridge manufacturing.

(c) The third is the step-up buyer who already has a game system and now wants something more sophisticated. Such a person might step up to computers which we will discuss later.

(d) Although the main turn of your business will come from kids, there is a potential market out there in older people. The business people of Japan who once patronized Pachinko parlors now are flocking to video arcades. Likewise we see more and more adults in video arcades in North America. These are your potential customers as well.

3. Video games buying

Here is a guideline to help you plan the video game business.

(a) When buying, be very careful. Video games are marketed the way records are. There are hits and there are dogs. Since game manufacturers will not take returns, select products carefully.

(b) Stock a large range of titles rather than a large number. Treat the business as a "hit" business. Of course, you will buy more of a sure hit.

(c) Display your games prominently. They need to be shown. Some dealers put games under glass counters. Some put them on shelves and take the risk from shoplifters.

(d) Create a demonstration area with two or three monitors for the types of game consoles you want to carry.

(e) Advertising is necessary to create consumer interest. Posters, buttons, mobiles, and banners are good. An effective sales promotion tool in video games is to hold regular competitions. Award trophies for good scores. You may involve media to carry out your coverage.

(f) Watch the market trends. If you find that the craze for a game is diminishing, you should promote it and sell out of it. Then stock only small quantities of it.

(g) Watch out for video games' biggest competitor — computers. Price reductions in computers are the main enemies of video game merchandisers. All the popular computers have the same capabilities as video game consoles and more.

b. COMPUTERS

Ever since the microchip was invented, computers have been commonplace in the world of business.

Now they have invaded many private homes in the form of personal home computers. They are everywhere. There are little ones you can take with you in your pocket, medium-size ones for your car, more complex ones for your home.

The growth in demand for personal home computers has influenced big computer giants like IBM to introduce the IBM Personal Computer. This has in turn sparked off a flurry of activity in the industry. The popularity of video games has also played a great part in promoting the popularity of personal home computers.

The writing is on the wall. If you are thinking of owning a video store (or if you already own one) you cannot afford to ignore the potential of computers. You must make a decision whether to stock home computers or not.

There are hundreds of books about computers. You should read several of them so that you understand how they work and which ones would be best for you to stock.

c. SATELLITE TV

This part of the electronics industry, like the video business, is growing fast. It is compatible with the video business in that it complements the home entertainment industry. Unit sales jumped from 100 to over 50,000 in five years. Prices have at the same time fallen drastically.

Satellite TV, sometimes referred to as TVRO (Television Receiver Only) will continue to grow at a great pace. Everywhere you go, whether urban or rural, you see satellite receiving dishes on roof tops or in back yards.

TVRO consists of three major components.

(a) *The antenna* receives microwave signals from satellites that circle the earth. This is the dish-like piece of equipment.

(b) *The Low Noise Amplifier (LNA)* amplifies the signals and filters them.

(c) *The receiver*, which processes the video and audio sections, is connected to the television set where the signals are presented for viewing.

Because satellite TV presents a wide variety of programming, there is a ready market for it. Some experts say that this industry will soon be one of the most favorable home entertainment industries in the world. The big market will be in rural areas where regular television programming is poor. In addition, satellite TV provides good quality pictures.

If you decide to stock satellite TV in your store, make sure you have the following at your disposal:

(a) A good roof or back yard that faces the center of the earth, away from major signal obstructions. (In North America, of course, it would face south.)

(b) A good compound or warehouse where you can stock the huge dishes safely and away from vandals.

(c) A good team of installers who have the knowledge to deliver and install the system.

Installation can present problems for inexperienced staff. They must know how to avoid interferences like trees or structures that shield the antenna from receiving full microwave signals. They must also be careful not to damage property. If not careful, the dish can cause a roof to collapse. Weather conditions can add to the difficulty in installations. Be wary of snow conditions where you install. Snow may be heavy and can cause a collapse of your installation.

You should insure your company against possible claims for property damage and personal injury.

Always include the installation price in your quotation when negotiating with a customer, and make sure you add enough because labor cost on installation can be very high. Check around the other TVRO suppliers and see how much they are quoting for installation. Sometimes it is possible to farm out installation to professional installers.

There are some risks involved in the satellite industry. Rural areas are exposed to satellite spacing legislation that is meant to protect the owners of satellite broadcast rights. This issue is confusing and even some people in the industry do not know what spacing is all about.

If you retail satellite dishes, you should recommend that consumers purchase a 12 foot dish that would still be legal if satellite spacing legislation is passed.

Another danger faced by the satellite business is the issue of signal scrambling. Home Box Office (HBO), North America's television service, has announced plans to scramble its signal to close off its service to satellite owners, many of whom purchased the systems in order to receive uncut recent movies. This will definitely hurt the satellite business. There is an alternative, however. Customers can get the same programming from pay services that are not scrambling their signals. Some experts say that if HBO scrambles their signals, other services will be born as alternatives. Already there are about nine other channels that show movies on satellite and there are other pay services doing the same thing as HBO.

Yet another danger that haunts the satellite business is the Direct Broadcast Satellite (DBS) system that features a few channels of prime programming from higher powered satellites. These satellites beam their signals at 100 watts rather than normal 5 watts allowed for smaller dish sizes. As a dealer you have to watch your stock so that you do not get caught with many unsold large dishes when DBS is taking off as the popular system to have.

11

RENTAL SYSTEMS

a. MOVIES

The system you devise for renting out your movies and equipment will depend on your floor plan, how much space you have, and your ideas on good marketing. To get you started on a few ideas that might suit your store, here are different arrangements you might want to try.

1. Vid-shelves

Vid-shelves are ready-made plastic shelves manufactured especially for movie jacket display; they can be purchased at a very low cost.

The advantage of displaying movies on the wall is that customers can handle the jacket, read the story lines and be more involved with the product.

The disadvantage of this display system is that it can be very untidy. Because of the many different sizes and combinations of jackets produced by different studios, the display area can look poor. You or someone on your staff will have to take the time to keep the jackets in good presentable order.

While you display the movie jackets on the wall, the actual prerecorded cassette is kept behind the counter and arranged in a systematic manner — either by numbers corresponding to a master list, or in alphabetical order. Most stores keep the prerecorded cassettes in protective plastic boxes to keep dust out of the cassette. These boxes can then be labeled, either by number or by title.

Have your customers bring the movie jacket to the counter when they want to rent. In that way, the rented out movie can be kept aside until the movie is rented. Create a section to display the jackets that are in the "out" category so that all your titles are displayed at all times.

Another alternative to this sytem is to stick labels on the jacket of the rented movie. The label will indicate that the movie is not available for rent that night. However, if you have a large library, you may find this system too difficult to keep up with.

When a movie is selected by a customer, you should have a method of recording it. The record should tell you who rented what title, and when, at what charge, and whether it has been paid for or not, and the amount of the deposit, if any. When the title is returned, there should be a system to indicate that it has, in fact, been returned.

Some movie clubs have a card for each member to record this information. To cross check the return of those movies that have been rented out, most stores have a system of recording them by title. Each title will have a separate card. (See Sample #8 and #9.)

SAMPLE #8
MEMBERSHIP CARD

VAL'S VIDEO SHOP

MEMBER'S NAME _____

MEMBERSHIP # _____ TEL. # _____

ADDRESS _____

DEPOSIT _____

DATE OF MEMBERSHIP _____

TITLE	**IN**	**OUT**	**PAID AMT.**
1. On Golden Pond	Jan. 13	Jan. 12	$4.00
2. The Thing	Jan. 14	Jan. 13	$4.00
3.			
4.			
5.			

SAMPLE #9
MOVIE CHECK LIST

TITLE: ON GOLDEN POND VHS

MEMBER	**OUT**	**IN**
1. Mr. John Smith	Jan. 7	Jan. 8
2. Mrs. F. Wong	Jan. 8	Jan. 9
3. Mr. Jon Doe	Jan. 9	Jan. 10
4.		
5.		

2. The movie board

The movie board is a display of trimmed movie jackets placed prominently onto a board. Circular disks underneath indicate whether the movie is available and in which format. You can code each movie by number and easily keep track of them this way.

If you have more than one copy of the title you can add disks to the hooks that are installed under the cut out jackets.

When a customer wants to rent a VHS copy of the title, he or she is asked to take the tags to the counter. The counter person will locate the appropriate title and off goes another rental. If no more tags are shown under the cut out jacket, it indicates to other customers that the particular title is unavailable in your store for that night.

This system is easy to run and has a professional look.

Cutting up the jackets poses a problem. If you buy a defective copy of a prerecorded cassette, you will need to replace it. Most distributors will want to submit the copy intact. Yet, if you have any influence over your distributor, you can make a switch. In other words, you give back the cassette without the jacket and get the good one without the cover in return.

This method takes a long time to prepare the titles for rental. After cutting up the jackets, they have to be displayed, numbers have to be assigned, and the actual cassette has to be catalogued in your inventory.

If you receive about a dozen movies, it will probably take about half an hour to get everything ready for rental, that is, if you have no interruptions. The sooner you put the titles out, the faster you will start making your capital back.

3. Behind the counter

This is a variation of the vid-shelf display method. Both prerecorded cassette and the jacket are placed together behind a long counter. The jacket is stood up while the prerecorded cassette is placed lying down on the shelf.

This method has the advantage of knowing what stock is in at a glance. If there is no prerecorded cassette where the jacket is, then the title has been rented. Your customer will know at once.

The disadvantage is that the customer will not be able to handle the jacket and read the storylines. Some stores have purchased movie review books to help eliminate this problem. However, the rating by the movie reviewers in these books may turn the customers away from some good video rental titles.

Another disadvantage is the need to purchase a long counter, which can be quite costly.

4. Space saver merchandiser

For stores that are short on space, the best way to merchandise movies titles is to cut up jackets as described in the movie board system. Because space is a problem, these cut up jackets can be displayed in large book-like foldable boards. This only takes up about four square feet of wall space with eight movie titles per board page. Each unit of boards may hold sixteen pages. Therefore, one unit can contain up to 128 jacket titles. If the total stock of movies amounts to, say, 500 VHS and 250 Beta, the store will need six units installed along a wall. In all, six units will take no more than 30 square feet of wall space. See the illustration on page 61 for an example of this merchandiser unit.

Another variation is to make a merchandiser unit that is free standing and can be rotated. This kind of merchandiser uses less floor space. See illustration below.

With the merchandisers, the method of rental recording will be the same as the movie board system. Of course, you may have variations of recording methods to suit your needs.

5. Catalogues

This system is also suitable for stores where space is at a premium.

In this method, jackets are not used at all. Instead, the titles available for rental are arranged in well prepared catalogues which customers may refer to.

By referring to the catalogue a customer can tell what movies are stocked, but they won't be able to tell whether they are in house for rent. The catalogues may be arranged in categories like drama, comedy, adventure, horror, etc.

A rotating floor stand movie jacket merchandiser

A wall movie jacket merchandiser with foldable book-like boards

6. Library rental cases

Whichever system you choose, you should protect your video cassettes from dust and damage by storing them in library cases.

There are many types of library cases. Some are suitable for both the VHS and Beta. But most stores use different sizes to differentiate between the two formats.

In selecting your library cases, choose only those that have hub extrusions. These extrusions keep the tape from running loose. Loose tape can get tangled in machines and possibly ruin them.

Usually case manufacturers make the cases in a number of colors. Select the color that will blend with your store colors. This will make your store look much more professional.

There are a number of good brands on the market. Their prices do vary, so shop around. Among the better known brands are Amaray, Blackbourn, Supreme, and Custom Cases.

7. Pre-viewing rentals

No matter which system you choose for your rental movies, always preview them — even for a few minutes — before you rent them out. The label on the cassette and everything else may say it is one movie, but a different one could be recorded on the cassette. It is much better for you to discover it than the customer at home.

b. MACHINE RENTALS

1. Regular rental

Most stores keep about 10 machines of a mixture of both formats for rental — usually for a short term. Daily rentals are most common because they are most profitable.

Your system of renting machines should incorporate a reservation book in which staff taking orders enter all details regarding the reservation. A typical reservation page could look like the one in Sample #10. Notice that there is provision for the reservation of movies as well.

VCR rentals can be very profitable. But you have to administer the whole business so as not to have any customer dissatisfaction. Customers who make reservations on machines and movies must be able to pick up their rental units and movies without having to wait too long for them. Many times dealers are careless in their operations and have made customers angry simply because they did not have enough to go around. It is poor policy to overbook your machines. On the contrary, you will find that you will need more machines than you own, especially on weekends.

2. Rent to buy

A good way to increase your business is to institute a lease-to-buy program for your machines. You may want to do this with a leasing company which supplies the funds, checks out the creditability of a potential customer, and also takes care of the collection of payments.

Here is how the program works. Suppose a VCR is priced at $1,000. You can rent it for $100 a month for 12 months. At the end of that time, the customer would own it for a total payment of $1,200. You make $200 on the rental/sale. This is in addition to the percentage you made on top of your cost of the VCR.

```
Price of VCR to customer      $1,000
Lease payments (12 months at $100)          $1,200
Cost of VCR                                 $  800
TOTAL PROFIT                                $  400
```

SAMPLE #10
MACHINE RENTAL FORM

DATE _____

NAME	VCR	MOVIES	FORMAT
	Sanyo		
	Panasonic		
	RCA		
	Hitachi		
	Sony		
	Quasar		

Another variation is to charge lower monthly payments, with a final "buy-out" payment at the end of the rental term. Suppose you charge $90 per month for 11 months. Total payments would bring it to $990. Buy-out of the VCR at end of the rental is $250. The total payment is therefore $1,240. Your profit is $440.

In order to provide this program, you must have a very good cash flow to carry the unpaid balances. In addition you should have a standard contract drawn up by a lawyer.

c. DEPOSITS ON RENTALS

Because the investment in VCRs is high, and the cost of movies prohibitive, much care must be taken to protect your money. Let's face it, there are crooks out there who will try to take your money in many devious ways.

To best protect yourself, get a deposit for the products you rent out. After all, you are giving a stranger a few hundred dollars tucked under his or her arm on complete trust. The deposit serves only as security, which in most circumstances does not come close to covering your costs.

Deposits may be in the form of cost-saving cash or you can ask for an imprint of a credit card. Have the customer sign the imprint, then (and this is very important) call the appropriate credit card office for an approval or authorization for an amount you think suitable for a deposit. Do not forget to note the authorization number on the imprint. Inform the customer that you will not submit the imprint — rather it will be the deposit. Most customers will not object to this method, although they have every right to refuse.

If all else fails, and you are still interested in making a few dollars for the big risks you are taking, you can check on a couple of things first. Get a signed personal check and take down driver's license number and a charge card number.

The best and safest bet is to insist on cold cash. The amount of the deposit is up to you.

12

MEMBERSHIP PLANS

Most video stores have a membership plan. What will you do? What are the advantages and disadvantages of having a membership plan?

a. ADVANTAGES

The most important advantage to a membership plan is that you can tie the customer down to your store. Membership plans can be for one month, one year, or lifetime. If you have signed a customer up for lifetime, you can be sure you will be seeing him or her in the store a good number of times.

Second, the fee charged for the membership is additional revenue for you. In fact, it provides immediate cash flow that you can use to buy new titles for your library. If your membership fee is $50 for one year, you can use that for one good movie. If you had 500 members, you would get 500 movies. You can be sure you will get about 500 good return customers.

b. DISADVANTAGES

One disadvantage of a membership plan is that you will probably not draw customers from far away. People who reside far away from your store will prefer to deal with a club nearer their home. If there are no clubs nearby, they will probably wait for one to be opened.

The other danger of having a membership plan is that another store nearby may not use one. You may find it hard to attract customers. The store that does not charge membership fees will have an advantage over you.

Survey your area and check out your competitors before making your decision. Even supermarkets are now beginning to rent movies.

c. MEMBERSHIP PRIVILEGES

What can a customer expect to get with a membership? You will have to sell the benefits of a membership plan in order to attract members to your store.

You might want to offer members several benefits, such as:
(a) 15% discount on equipment purchases
(b) Lower movie rental charges
(c) Movie reservations privilege
(d) 10% discount on accessories

I know of some clubs where it costs nothing to join. But there are no special privileges for such members. Movie rentals are the same for members as for others who walk through the door. The only advantage of this system is that you have customers' names in a file for mailing lists.

Membership plans should be flexible. You should be able to change the operational methods as trends dictate. However, the charges should remain firm. You cannot have one customer paying $30 for a membership and another paying $50. Yet your membership benefits should be revised often to stimulate interest. For example, if you get a good buy on blank tape you should let your members know that you are passing on some good deals to them.

There are many ways to sell memberships. Some stores sell without any gimmicks. Some sell memberships but also give away T-shirts, or pop, or free movie rentals. One good promotion is to include a discount coupon on their first purchase of an accessory. That way you are sure you will be generating some activity in your accessory business.

d. THE MEMBERSHIP CARD

If you opt for a membership system for your club, you will need certain documentation to tell one member from another, and members from non-members.

Most membership clubs will provide a membership card to a member that states the rules of membership. For example, you might want to include the following membership conditions on the card:

(a) Videotape must be used only by the cardholder for personal, non-commercial purposes

(b) Cardholder will be responsible for any damage or misuse of videotape

(c) Cardholder agrees that he or she will not duplicate the videotape, loan it to others or use it in violation of copyright or other laws

(d) Return of videotape in good condition by due date must be made before another videotape can be rented

(e) Cardholder agrees to pay an additional charge of $5 for any videotape not returned by due date.

Some clubs require the customer's photograph to be on the card. This allows for easy identification of members and helps with security problems.

e. MOVIE RESERVATIONS

Most customers like to be able to reserve movies. But the implementation of a reservation system may be a problem. If run poorly you can make more enemies than friends.

If you do have a movie reservation system, make sure you draw up a good system with strict rules for both staff and customers to observe. You are the one who must see that the system is adhered to.

Here are some typical rules governing a movie system:

(a) Reservations may be made by phone or in person 24 hours before pickup time.

(b) No more than two titles may be reserved at any one time.

(c) Reserved movies must be picked up by closing time or else one day's rental will be assessed to the person who reserved the movie.

(d) All reserved movies must be returned by 5 p.m. the next day.

When initiating your system, keep good records so that there will be no mixups. As soon as a reservation is made, ensure that the person's name and phone number and the movie titles are recorded in your reservation book. The book will have a page for each calendar day. Before you agree to a title reservation, make sure that the title is not already promised for someone else. When the reserved title is back in your store, phone the customer for pick up.

13

ADVERTISING AND PROMOTION

a. ADVERTISING

Advertising, in one form or another, is a must for your store. Good advertising will bring you your customers and persuade them to buy. You should apportion part of your operating budget to advertising.

Here's how to make sure you reach and motivate the people you want to sell to — and that your advertising money will go where it will do you the most good in your market.

First write down and organize everything you want your advertising to accomplish for your business within the year: the markets you want to reach and the sales volume you want to generate.

You may have three or four basic objectives that you want your advertising to help you meet.

Whatever you decide, write them down, both major and minor objectives, with dates, numbers, or percents precisely spelled out. This gives you some basic goals and an idea of your timing.

Pinpoint your audience by categories in their order of importance to your selling effort. Who are your most important customer groups? Are they the people who just rent movies, or regular buyers of accessories?

Your audiences will vary in their makeup and in their importance to you according to the population, your geographic area and the mix of people or businesses you wish to serve.

Your own sales and delivery records, credit records, or other active customer records can help you pinpoint who your customers are, what they buy, and where they're located.

Next, choose the media or formats that will best help you reach your market specifically and consistently. Remember, each format has specific advantages and limitations. Be sure to choose a *balance* of media that will give you the fullest possible market coverage for the time and money you've allocated for your campaigns.

You may want to use newspapers backed by selected direct mail, transit cards in your market area, and radio campaigns for special sales.

No one medium will reach *all* of your market regularly. You need a good mix of media to ensure that your advertising is selling for you all the time, to as many prospects as possible.

Here's how the media mix can best be used to build traffic and sales for you.

1. Newspapers

Newspapers are a top choice for a timely or newsworthy ad. This can mean the announcement of a new product, a special store sale or in-store demonstrations. Your newspaper ad should tie into a special sale, the opening of a new location, new services, or events such as holidays.

If you don't consider yourself creative or do not have creative talent available, try a discount or special-offer coupon. These days, there are no better attention-getters for budget-conscious consumers.

2. Magazines

Small business people have generally avoided advertising in large magazines because of the high cost. There are, however, an increasing number of smaller regional and city magazines that offer a good new investment potential.

The new city magazines, in particular, have been working to attract more new business from local small business. But before you select a regional edition or local magazine, be sure to find out how many of your potential customers read it. Ask the salesperson for circulation figures, and what groups of people those figures represent.

3. Radio

With radio, it's important to know the demographics (the make-up) of your target market. If your prospects are mostly men, you will want to place your commercials during shows that have predominantly male audiences. Choose your station carefully, too.

4. Television

There is no need to dismiss television as too costly any more. Though prime time may be too expensive, spot commercials aired late at night or during the day can be affordable.

Cable TV networks can offer you an exciting and reasonably priced advertising alternative.

Check with your station salesperson about how much production help and services you can get in preparing your scripts and visuals for television spots. Keep your visuals as simple and inexpensive as possible, and check the message for clarity and completeness.

Make sure you run your spots adjacent to the programs most likely to attract the viewers to whom you want your message delivered.

5. Yellow pages

Unlike the other media discussed, the yellow pages is unique in that it is actually a consumer's guide that prospects refer to once they've made up their minds to buy.

For businesses having difficulty coordinating advertising plans and monitoring their effectiveness, the yellow pages offers a unique opportunity to stretch your ad dollar.

Because your yellow pages ad will be listed among other video retailers, promoting your special or unique services is essential. You can also use an attractive ad that will be eye-catching on the page.

6. Co-op advertising

Cooperative advertising, also known as "co-op," is a process in which two or more parties share the costs of advertising or promotion. The two parties could be a manufacturer and a retailer (or salesperson), two retailers or two business owners. They are cooperating by pooling money to buy more advertising or promotional materials than one party could get alone. It is a very valuable tool for the video retailer who wants to make every advertising dollar count. Using co-op advertising will enlarge your advertising dollar.

Co-op advertising tends to stimulate floor traffic and product movement.

If you are interested in co-op advertising, you should ask the manufacturers the following questions:

(a) What is the basis for accrual of co-op fund?

(b) Is there a time period in which accrual is based? (Most manufacturers will only allow accrual over a calendar year.)

(c) What percentage of the advertising rate does your co-op program cover?

(d) When should claims be submitted?

(e) What requirements are necessary regarding the use of company logos and brand names?

(f) Are camera ready ads available?

7. Mailing list

The purpose of having a mailing list is to have a list of names to distribute your messages. These messages may be sales promotions, specials, newsletters, or even Christmas cards.

The mailing list should be started from day one. Make one staff member responsible for it and you will have one job less. Every now and then, update the list.

8. Advertising program

Most good video retailers will plan their advertising program a year ahead of time. This gives them lots of time to talk to representatives, get the necessary funds from co-op advertising programs and contact media before the actual advertisement appears. It will also give time to order the appropriate products for the campaigns.

Advertising schedules are not meant to be rigid. In fact if market trends demand changes, the advertising strategy should change likewise. It is a good idea to review your schedule every few months.

b. PROMOTION

Sales promotion is simply any sales activity that *supplements* personal selling or advertising and helps to make them more effective. It includes special events, demonstrations, promotion kits, displays, theme sales, clear-out sales, new product promotions or service promotions, and much more.

Sales promotion is out of the ordinary routine of sales efforts. It is the special push you give to promote sales of specific products or services over a short and clearly set period of time. Whatever sales promotion you plan should fit in with your overall marketing plan.

Sales promotion can be used to:

(a) Build store traffic or find new clients/customers for your business.

(b) Extend selling seasons on seasonal items and services.

(c) Clear out old or slow-moving inventories.

(d) Broaden your business area or customer base.

(e) Meet a specific competitive situation.

(f) Increase the value per order of your sales.

(g) Reclaim lost or dormant accounts.

(h) Introduce new products, lines or services you offer.

(i) Build customer goodwill and involvement in your business.

Here are some promotion ideas that may help your video outlet.

1. Grand opening

You open your store only once so it should be a grand affair. Offer special prices to customers. You want to make so much noise that people are attracted to the opening.

You might get local theatre groups or high school kids and dress them up in attractive costumes. Buy some inflated balloons and give them away to kids. Make the affair a festival. People like that.

When planning your grand opening, incorporate it with your advertising campaign. Use your local paper and local radio station to announce the sales available on opening day.

One very important point: do not have a grand opening announcement unless you feel strongly that your store is ready for it. Nothing is worse than a half ready store that is open for business. You will just have a lot of dissatisfied customers that will not return.

2. Commander board

This is a huge display board that you can set up outside your store on a temporary basis. You can display sale messages on it.

The display advertising board will draw the attention of passing traffic and let everyone know that there is now a new video store in the area. Commander boards can be rented for a couple months or longer. The length of time you want to keep it depends on your requirements.

Before you rent the board, check with city hall about limitations on the location of such boards. Many authorities do not allow them at all. Some say they must be on private property away from traffic. But check first. Also check with your landlord. Other tenants in the same building may object to it.

Commander boards are an effective means to draw attention to a new store.

3. "Ladies," "senior citizens," or "members" night

Make one day a week a special night for one section of your market. Let members of that group rent two movies for the price of one. During slack times, you can broaden your categories to include everyone.

4. 99¢ deal

Some stores have effectively made 99¢ deals the talk of the town. For 99¢ per movie customers can watch all they want on certain days. This not only increases business on a slow day, but brings in potential customers for other days at regular rates.

5. Kids' deals

During the summer holidays kids will be in your stores more often, and parents will be trying to keep them occupied. Make specials and promotions attractive to children. Discount general movies, for example, or offer short term day-time only rentals at a two for one price.

6. Birthday deals

Tell your customers if they rent a VCR and two movies, you will present them with a birthday gift comprised of an assortment of balloons, candy, party hats, candles, etc.

This promotion works well, but the costs are high and could trim your profits. Your promotion will have to be properly costed before you implement it. You cannot provide the rental of a VCR and two movies for a day for, say, $15 when your gift amounts to $5. Your price tag will have to be higher.

7. The new arrival board

If you went out today and purchased a few movies for your stock, how would you let your customers know that you now have those in your store?

Make out a list and post it in a prominent place. Mark the list NEW ARRIVALS. The results will be tremendous.

Many dealers complain that certain titles are poor movers. Usually it is only because they have done nothing to advertise the fact that they have those titles in stock.

If you make a well designed new arrival board, it will add some class to your store. Make your board of a material you can write on. A chalkboard will do fine, but make sure it is cleaned with water and wiped dry each time you use it. A dirty board will look messy.

See illustration for an example of a New Arrivals Board.

Some stores have a free-standing console for their new arrivals. This can be very effective, and can draw attention of customers very easily. An illustration of such a console is on page 75.

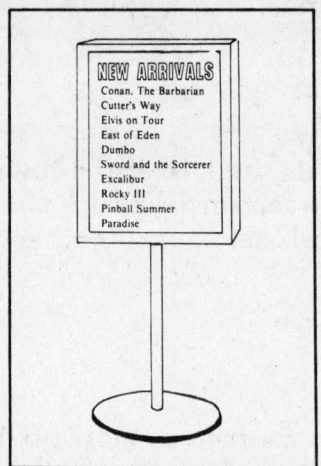

A new arrivals board

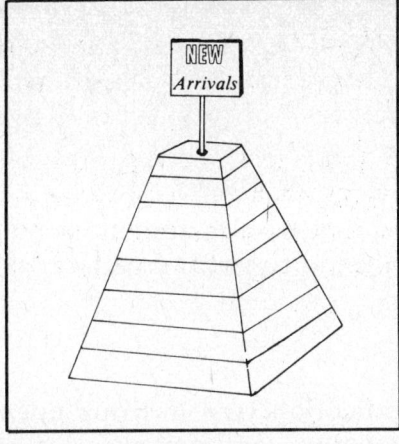

A new arrivals console

9. Staff's choice

People are like sheep. In a video store, you should play the role of the shepherd by guiding them with suggestions.

Make your suggestions in the form of a staff's choice board. Every day ask one staff member to pick a movie that does not rent out very well. Your intention is to turn over that movie more often so that your investment pays off faster. Place the movie jacket at a good location on the counter. Label the jacket in bold letters STAFF'S CHOICE. This will attract customers to the movie.

This idea has been used by supermarkets with great success, and it can work in a video store too. The illustration below will help you make one up. It does not cost very much.

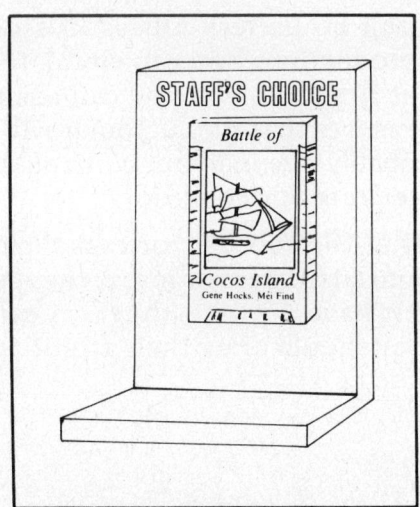

Counter top staff's choice stand

8. Posters

Posters can help decorate your store and at the same time sell something for you. Posters are your silent salesperosn. They stimulate sales and studios give them out readily at no charge. There are, however, poster stores all over the continent that sell specialty posters that can have a great selling effect. Posters should be handled with care because they cost a lot of money.

One word of caution — if you do not have a certain movie, do not display the poster that advertises it unless you intend to get it at a later date.

10. Newsletters

An essential marketing and communication tool in your operation will be a member newsletter. This is the best medium of communication between you and your customers. In fact by reading the store's newsletter, your own staff members will learn about your sales specials, the rental policies, store hours, etc. The newsletter may be published once a month, bi-monthly or quarterly, depending on your budget.

It gives you a chance to tell customers regularly what is new in your store. New arrivals and new products should make it into your newsletter. If you have new staff, tell customers that too. Write a blurb about the person. This is the place to sell your staff member before he or she sells him/herself.

Dealers who do not have the time or the necessary writing skills or the inclination to produce a presentable newsletter can participate in a generic newsletter called *Video Showcase*. It is a well-written, well-produced publication. You can place personal and customized store messages with your store name in it. Such newsletters will go a long way in promoting your store's image.

The address of *Video Showcase* is 41 West 10th Street, New York, NY 10011.

Any newsletter you produce will be useless unless it is well distributed. Circulation is as important as the production. You can circulate the newsletter the expensive way, that is, mailing it first class. Or you can use third class mail. Mailing, I find, is most effective. It ensures that the customer will receive it at the door. Whether it is read or not is probably beyond your control. Check with your post office for any special newsletter rates or conditions.

Some dealers leave newsletters at the counter for casual pick up. If you do that, make sure that staff give them to customers or insert them with the movies or other sales. In fact if staff members have the time, they may care to discuss the newsletters with the customers. They should draw their attention to the specials you have offered.

11. Special effects

Innovative special effects can distinguish one store from another. One store I know spent a few hundred dollars decorating a special horror section. There were goblins, monsters, bats, and other wax figures. Track lights highlighted horror movies, and played ghostly sound effects in the section. The store was a big hit in that city. Every kid in the neighborhood had to see the store, and naturally parents went along too.

Another store had a special kids section with Cinderella and Disney characters. Flowers and plants filled that section. The store was popular because it had class and it was different.

Still another video store lured customers with old-time movie theatre chairs, pop, chewing gum, and free popcorn. This gave the store a cinema atmosphere.

There are many other innovations you can use. It is fun to come up with your own ideas and try them. The more ideas you come up with, and use, the more successful you are going to be.

12. Special events

Since you are in the show business, you must be aware of the special events that concern the business. Big events like the Academy Awards must be of interest to you. The stars and films that receive nominations and win the awards will be the talk of many consumers for weeks after the event. The stars who made it to the top will attract attention from consumers. The movies they starred in will rent better. Take note of the winning films. When they finally become available to you, you must pay special attention to them. These will be your big renters.

Besides the Academy Awards, you should be aware of the Cannes Film Festival and the Emmy Awards. When you have information regarding the awards, your customers will appreciate your informing them in the store. How you do it is up to you. You could use posters, newsletters, or word of mouth. They will make pretty good conversation pieces and spur sales. Keep abreast with the business and you will be one up on your competition.

13. Change displays

To increase customer and staff interest, you should change your displays fairly often. A new arrangement makes things look different and customers will notice movies or pieces of equipment they overlooked before.

14
MARKETING YOUR VIDEO STORE

Marketing is: product, price, place, and promotion. You decide on a product to be the commodity that you can exchange for money. Then you must have a price that is agreed upon between the seller and the buyer. And you must get the product to the right place at the right price at the right time which brings promotion into play.

Marketing is more than advertising or merchandising. It involves all the activities that make a product a customer will buy and get it at the right price at the right time.

In retailing video products, you have to market *your* product and *your* store. A good deal of pre-selling has already been done for you. For example, all manufacturer advertising of equipment is being carried out at great intensity. In any video magazine you will see advertisements by Sony, Panasonic, and others. They have created customer demand for you. Now when you buy their products your turn comes trying to sell to the public.

a. SELLING

The most important part of marketing is selling. Selling involves coming into contact with customers to induce them to buy. In the last chapter, we discussed advertising which will help bring customers to your store where you will get a chance to induce them to buy.

You should develop qualities to ensure a friendly atmosphere and to generate sales. You must learn to be patient because you cannot force your customers to pull out their money. You will have to try many ways to persuade customers to part with their money in exchange for your goods.

You must also be sensible. Common sense is very important in this business. If you can sense that a customer is waiting for you to close the sale and you do not do it, you will have lost the sale and perhaps the customer.

You should also be observant. Observant sales people always come up tops in any sales seminar. A sharp sales person is able to gauge when the right time is to close the sale.

While being all the above, you also need to possess the right attitude about your work. Don't be too easily discouraged if you lose a couple of sales.

Attitude is difficult to change once it gets into a rut. Start with a positive attitude and keep it.

Customers do not like buying or associating with a gloomy or grumpy sales person. No one wants to be associated with failures, so look successful.

You should be able to speak well about your product, but you must also have the ability to listen. Customers go to stores to buy products, not listen to grand stories of how great you are. A good listener will soon learn what a customer's needs are.

Last you should be honest. If you are dishonest, you will soon lose the confidence of your customers. If a product is, in your opinion, not suitable for the customer, say so. You will immediately win the customer's trust.

b. HOW TO DEMONSTRATE VIDEO EQUIPMENT

There are no hard and fast rules in demonstrating video equipment. You will have a different approach from other sales people. But you will have the same objective — to close the sale.

A demonstration is only a tool for a sales person. It is a tool leading to your sale. As long as you remember this, you are well on your way to closing the sale.

When a customer walks through the door into your store always presume that he or she is there to buy. Once you presume that, part of your sale is complete.

Suppose you are preparing to sell a VCR. Here is a step-by-step procedure.

1. Know the product

Before you can demonstrate a VCR you must know the product. Take one home and fiddle with it for a good length of time and read the instructions. Familiarize yourself with the various features of the machine. Learn about the advantages of programming. Learn how to set up the timer. Try to patch up a stereo sound simulator while you are at it.

The more you learn about the VCR the easier your presentation will be, and consequently the more confidence your customer will have in you.

2. Explain the product

Do not switch the set on right away for the customer. First explain what the machine is. Tell your customer in brief terms what a VHS is versus Betamax. Show the two tape formats.

3. Show the product

Now put the power on for both the VCR and the television and explain how you set the time. While doing this, switch off the television set. It may distract your customer's attention. Have the customer do it as well. Get the customer involved in handling the machine. The more a customer handles it, the better he or she will like it.

Explain the timer functions and programming. Show the various steps and various options. Go very slowly here because it can be confusing.

Switch the television set on again and show how you tune in the converter and the various channels. Show what the machine is capable of doing. Stay away from technical terms as much as possible. You aren't there to impress the customer about how much you know, but on what the equipment can do. The majority of customers do not care what the power consumption is. They care about things like the capabilities of picture search, slow motion, the timer, remote control, and so on.

4. Ask the customer

Now ask the customer what type of films he or she would like to view. After the selection, pop in the movie and let it run for about a minute or two. Show how the tracking features at this time. Also demonstrate the hard and soft picture features. Persuade the customer to follow you.

Stop the movie and substitute one that you have recorded off the television on the fast speed. A sports program would be excellent. Demonstrate the features of still pause, fast search, fast forward, and rewind. Now play the program for another couple of minutes and leave the customer alone for that length of time.

5. Close the sale

Ask the customer, "Do you want to know anything more about the recorder?" If your customer has questions, answer them intelligently. Ask if the customer would like another demonstration. If the answer is no, ask "Is there anything that you do not like about the VCR?" If the answer to this is no, you can close the deal.

Keep all your order forms, sales slips, purchase orders, selling materials, and specification sheets organized and ready to use near by. Include any advertising reprints, brochures, testimonials or other leave-behinds that can help you make the sale.

Close the sale only if it is a good deal for your prospect. Salesmanship is *not* the art of manipulating people into making bad decisions, conning someone, or getting them to buy products or services they don't need or can't afford. Nor is it pushing poor service, shoddy products or sloppy workmanship.

If the sale doesn't work for your prospect, it doesn't work for you either. You may get their money once, but you'll never get it again.

A customer who is really interested in the machine is waiting for you to make the next move.

Here are some closing lines used by successful video retailers:

(a) Now, would that be 20 feet of coaxial cable or 50 feet? (Coaxial cables are so inexpensive you can always throw extra in with the sale.)

(b) Do you need a stereo sound simulator (or headcleaner) to go with the set?

(c) Do you need financing on the set?

(d) Do you want to take the set with you or shall I deliver it?

(e) I think you are going to enjoy watching this movie tonight. (Throw in the movie rental with the deal.)

(f) Or the famous closing line "Will that be cash or charge?"

d. FOLLOW-UPS

Renowned Joe Girard, acknowledged as the best salesman in the world, devised a good follow-up system. He made sure all his prospective buyers were contacted immediately. If he did not close on a deal after the initial sales presentation, he made follow-up calls. Usually follow-up calls brought customers back for another demonstration where there was another chance for him to close the sale.

Not only did Joe Girard have a follow-up system for prospective customers, he also kept an account file for his old customers. He sent them reminders on servicing their vehicles, sent them birthday cards, and called them after six months of the sale to ask if everything was all right with their car. And after three years he called again to check if the customer was ready to buy again.

You can apply the same style to your video business. If you carry out a good follow-up system, you will attain very high sales repeats and strong referrals from those customers you have sold to.

The names of old customers should be kept in a card file. In it you should keep details about the type of equipment purchased, dates purchased, birthdays, addresses, and so on. And of course do not forget the phone numbers. Check the file every day. It will not take long to send a reminder or a birthday card. The effects of a customer receiving such things go a long way.

Use your calling card for follow-up. Your card is your best advertising. Make sure you go to a good printer and a professional graphic designer for a good design. A good looking card will be kept for a long time. If ordinary and unattractive, calling cards will be cast aside before too long.

15
DAILY OPERATIONS

a. HOURS OF OPERATION

Every retailer wonders how many hours a store should be open. Does it pay to stay open 12 hours a day and hope that the extra business will compensate for the amount it costs for heat, electricity, etc?

If you are located in a mall, your choice is probably very limited. Most mall administrations dictate your hours of operation. However, if you have an outside entrance to a mall, you can, with the agreement of mall management, operate on your own hours.

At other store locations you can select your hours to suit consumer needs. Most video stores do not open early in the day. Most open at 10:00 a.m. When you open that early, you have a better chance of renting a movie early with the hope that it will be returned by the afternoon for another turn. Most video stores close at 9 p.m., though some stay open much later.

To ascertain hours best for your store, have your visitors complete a very simple survey. Ask the first 100 customers to complete a simple questionnaire on their shopping habits. The results will tell you your best operating hours.

Always stick to your hours of operation once a decision is made. I have seen totally confused customers when a store varies its hours from one season to the other. Not only does it give customers an excuse for returning movies late, it creates ill feelings and frustration. Nothing is more unpleasant than to make an effort to get to a store at 8:30 p.m. to find that the closing time has been changed to 8:00 p.m. Likewise, if you decide to open at 9:00 a.m. make sure you open at 9:00 a.m. Not at 9:01 a.m. or 9:05 a.m.

Your customers expect you to be a professional business person. You should be in your store a good half hour prior to opening. The extra half hour gives you time to do regular housekeeping chores, book work, cash balances, put up posters, etc. That will leave you the rest of the day to do more productive work like selling and renting.

b. GOOD HOUSEKEEPING

The appearance of your store is important to customer satisfaction. If your store is in disrepair, chances are your stock will be in poor shape. Your equipment will be mistreated, there will be scratches in your movies, and your customers will think you are out to make a fast buck.

You do not have to spend a lot of money to keep your operation clean and presentable. If you develop a procedure whereby each one of your staff is involved, you do not have to fuss about housekeeping.

Make sure you draw up a schedule and post it on the staff bulletin board. When drawing up a schedule ensure that everyone does a fair share. Do not forget that washrooms (even though you may have to do it yourself) must also be cleaned. Store front cleanliness must not be neglected. If the store front is littered, it creates a bad impression.

c. CUTTING COSTS

In retailing, or for that matter, in any business, there are always ways to cut costs. These costs are your expenses and are most important at the start of a new business.

Fixed costs like taxes, rent and depreciation are uncontrollable costs. But out of pocket costs like stationery, receipt books, and furniture can be controlled.

Costs that can be controlled must be reviewed regularly. The lower your costs are while carrying out business, the higher your net profit will be.

There are some controllable costs that you must be careful about when trying to minimize expenses. These are costs that relate closely to productivity like salaries, wages, and commission. You should pay your staff reasonably well so that you attract good people, and keep them.

If certain projects can be done by your own staff, and done well, you should do such projects inhouse instead of farming out projects to freelancers or contractors. Sometimes staff can surprise you when called upon to do certain tasks. Usually one or two staff members can look after merchandising, for example.

Limiting long distance phone calls is another cost cutting measure. You will be surprised at accumulated costs of telephone expenses if uncontrolled.

You should also take care not to allow yourself the luxury of too much entertainment expense. Usually sales representatives have expense accounts from their companies. If they take you out to lunch, it is their privilege to do so and you should feel honored. However, the return lunch by you is not entirely necessary. If the sales representative's products are useful to your store, and if they appear to have a good potential, you can say thank you by ordering the product.

In closing, there will be many areas in your operation where costs can be cut or minimized. If you are consistently looking out for them, it will become a habit. If you look after the pennies, dollars will follow.

d. DAILY SALES SUMMARY

Every day sales must be tabulated and posted in a daily sales summary book. The information should be posted in categories such as movies, VCRs, accessories, etc. (See Sample #11.) This will be a very useful tool to you when deciding what you should purchase more of when buying time arrives. It also tells you where your weak points are and where you should concentrate more effort.

The day's total must be used for your cash reconciliation.

SAMPLE #11
DAILY SALES SUMMARY

SALES						
Date	VCR	Movies	Accessories	Video Games	Others	Total
1 2 3 ↓ 31 Total						

RENTALS						
Date	VCR	Movies	Video Games	TVs	Others	Total
1 2 3 ↓ 31 Total						

e. CASH RECONCILIATION

Every retail store must have a cash reconciliation system that is done at the end of each shift. The purpose of this exercise is to match the sales rung up at your cash register with the actual cash on hand in the till.

The method is simple. Suppose at the end of the day you tally the following:

Expenses	$1.20	Sales indicated on tape	$1102.56
Cash in hand	1201.36	Float for the day	100.00
	$1202.56		$1202.56
			$0
Balance			0

You should arrive at a zero balance every day.

Sometimes expenses will create balancing problems. If you have purchased anything (goods or services), make sure receipts are kept together and accounted for during the reconciliation.

Void sales will also create similar problems if not accounted for. When counting your cash in hand, do not forget to include checks and charge card sales. Most retail operations insist on staff marking charge card sales on a charge card summary sheet as the sale is being rung up. This is one method of lessening the work for the person who does the reconciliation.

f. BANKING

Banking procedures must be established early in your store operation. Because you are dealing with money, security is of prime importance. Arrange with your bank for wallets and drop in privileges at the bank after office hours. When going to the bank, do not make your deposits every day at the same time. In other words, take a different route and at different times each day. Do not make it a planned pattern.

Make your deposits every day. The quicker you get your money into your account, the lower your debt load will be and the higher your cash flow. In the long run, a good sum of interest can be saved by regular deposits.

g. ACCOUNTING

Whether you have an accounting background or not you know that all businesses, big or small, must keep accounting books. If you do not, you will end up in a lot of trouble with the tax department. Mundane things like receipts, sales slips, bills, and invoices must be maintained and kept in proper order. If you know no bookkeeping, attend some classes or read a book. (See *Basic Accounting for the Small Business,* another book in the Self-Counsel Series.) Or you could delegate the job to one of the staff who has bookkeeping knowledge.

Whatever the case may be, I urge you to keep your books up-to-date and not let one week slip by. As soon as you let this go by, work accumulates and you will soon be doing catch up which is no fun. It is like keeping your mailing list up to date. You have to do it regularly.

Talk to your accountant. He or she can, for a small fee, devise a bookkeeping system for your store. If you already own a micro-computer you can purchase an accounting and bookkeeping software program to suit your business operations.

Your accountant will give you good advice on things to look out for with regard to your tax situation and ways to minimize your taxable income. You should keep and document all receipts, parking expenses, telephone expenses, restaurant receipts, etc. You will be amazed at the total at the end of the year. One year my total parking expenses came to a total of $246.45. Now that does not look like much, but it is $246.45 less added to my taxable income. If your store is in a heavy traffic area where parking is impossible unless you rent space, your parking expenses could be high.

How do you keep tabs on parking expenses when you cannot get receipts? Keep a log book in your car. It takes no more than three seconds to jot each entry down. Such proof may be requested by your tax department, although they usually accept small sums because it may cost them more to question such expenses unless they are extraordinarily high.

You can do the same thing with your telephone calls made from public phone booths. Keep a diary where you can jot down minor expenses like these. At the end of each month, make out a personal expense statement and attach all receipts to it. Your bookkeeper, or your accountant, would like these in proper order for the ease of posting entries and computations. At the same time your office and store expenses could be tabulated and matched each month. Such totals must be entered in your general ledger.

Keep in touch with your accountant. Some business people view accountants with some prejudice. They always think of taxes when they think about their accountants. But actually your accountant should work on your side. He or she should look after your financial well being. Sometimes accountants know of certain developments in the world of finance well before the average person does. They often have tips on interest rates, stocks, real estate, tax shelters, etc.

In conclusion, the more regularly you keep your books the less the work load and cost in the end. Accounting and bookkeeping are necessary evils in business yet very important for business decisions.

16
EVALUATING AND SELLING YOUR VIDEO STORE

There are many reasons you may want to sell your video store. But when the time comes it is a major decision on your part.

The most difficult step in selling (or buying) a business is probably determining what the business is worth. You will have to make a series of decisions. Yet before you take your first step and hire a real estate sales person to do the selling for you, or advertise in the business section of the newspaper, the value of your store must be established. The value must be a reasonable one that is acceptable to you, as seller, and the buyer.

Even before a value can be put on your store, a few things must be done.

(a) Clean up your store. Put a new coat of paint on the walls and steam clean the carpet. Make sure the store is looking its best.

(b) Do some homework. Find out more about your competition and what they are doing. See where your store stands in terms of potential and current standing.

(c) Check with city hall to see if another major development project is in the works in your store's vicinity. A new subdivision or a new apartment block would mean more customers in the future for a new owner.

Armed with the store information you will have more ammunition when negotiations come. In other words, the more you know about your market the better the deal you may make for yourself.

a. VALUATION METHODS

There are two basic methods of determining the value of a business:

(a) The first is based on the expectations of future profits and the return on investment (ROI).

(b) The second is based on the value of the assets at the time of negotiations.

The first method is preferable because it pays attention to market trends, growth, sales, and profits. It also takes into consideration the capitalized value of the business. And last, but not least, it considers the future expectations of the return on investment. Both seller and buyer will be looking at these factors.

The second method assumes that the assets will be used in the business by the buyer. Where assets like furniture and fixtures and inventory are considered, they will be used by the buyer. However, this method does not consider the future of the business. It determines asset values only as they relate to the present.

Of the two methods, the second is more commonly applied. It is an easier method because it is dealing with assets — something tangible. But it does not mean it is more reliable than the first. The projections needed to value future business can cause problems in negotiations.

Earlier, I said that before you advertise the store for sale you will have to do some homework. One piece of work you will certainly have to do is to draw up a pro forma statement (projected statement) on income and profit and loss for the next 12 months. In order to get to the statement you must have sales forecasts, estimated cost of goods sold to run concurrently with your sales forecast, and, of course, a matching estimated operating expense. There is no escape. If your potential buyer is a sharp one, you will be asked for the pro forma statement.

What is the value of a pro forma statement? It reflects the net profit you believe will be possible in the next 12 months. It gives the buyer an idea what to expect from the business should he or she buy it. The buyer will also be making a similar forecast statement that will be more critical and conservative than yours. Because the buyer is concerned about the future, he or she will be analyzing the actual profit and loss statement and also those of the past years, if any. Like you, the buyer will have studied the trading area to get a handle on the economic conditions of that vicinity. He or she will also have talked discreetly with your competition at some stage.

b. HOW TO FORECAST SALES

The most important part of your pro forma statement is the forecast of future sales. The more accurate you are, the more confident you will be when negotiating.

Forecasting your sales will require you to use past actual figures. Go back to your daily sales summaries and your monthly sales summaries to get actual annual figures by category. The further you go back, the better the trend you can extract out of them.

Using the trend as a back-up, you can forecast the future with more certainty. However, all forecasts are uncertain, and the longer you forecast your sales, the more uncertain it will be. You cannot control the external economic conditions even though you can put some control internally.

How long a forecast should you make for the prospective buyer? Perhaps the best way to approach the length of the forecast is in terms of the expected return on investment. Suppose the buyer expects to bring in 20% return on investment. The investment therefore should pay out in five years. It appears logical then to make a projection for the next five years.

When forecasting your sales, take into consideration general economic conditions of the country and the influences of other countries. Also consider industry changes in the video business. Many methods of forecasting sales can be used. I advocate using past performance and established trade. When projecting sales figures, always make the assumption that no market factors will greatly influence sales performance more in the future than in the past. Work from the bottom up.

If the growth of the second year over the first year is 5%, and the third over the second is 7%, take the average (which is 6%) and project a 6% growth in the first projected year over the third actual year, and 6% recurring after that.

Note that no forecasting method can set any value on external market conditions because there is no guarantee that those conditions will carry over into the future.

c. RISK AND RETURN ON INVESTMENT

Any buyer who wants to invest in a business will be concerned with getting a fair return on money invested. What is a fair rate of return? Naturally the more risk, the more gain. A buyer will be trying to gauge the risk factor of the video store you now own.

In trying to establish that, the buyer will be projecting the profits as far into the future as possible. He or she will analyze the profit-making capability of your store. Naturally the buyer will visit your store many times and observe traffic through it.

In the end, the buyer will consider the risk factor — maximizing it and at the same time minimizing the acceptable rate on return on investment. In minimizing acceptable return on investment, the buyer will be able to place the risk in perspective. In most small businesses the risk factor is fairly high. A fair or adequate risk return of a small business is usually between 20 to 25% return.

d. HOW TO VALUE A VIDEO STORE BY CAPITALIZING FUTURE EARNINGS

The price paid by the buyer for your store should be based on the capitalized value of future earnings, *not* on the purchase of assets. Profits are made by utilizing assets; assets purchased are only incidental to the future profits of the store.

Capitalized value is the value that would bring the earnings at a specified rate of interest. If the risk is high the rate is high. Above, I mentioned between 20 to 25% rate. The capitalized value is determined by dividing the annual profit by the specified rate of return (expressed as a decimal).

For example: assume that future profits for the next 5 years averages $20,000 per year. What then should the sale price be? If the buyer invested the money and expects to recover the initial investment in 4 to 5 years, at the projected earnings of $20,000 per year, the sale price should be between $80,000 to $100,000. To make the same $20,000 profit, the buyer would have to invest $200,000 in a government savings bond that pays 10% interest.

e. HOW TO VALUE YOUR STORE ON THE BASIS OF ASSET APPRAISAL

Because the first method of valuing business is more complicated and takes more work, most businesses are transacted on the basis of what the company has in assets. It is not a recommended method, but it is easier. If you have to use it, take note of the following suggestions:

1. Assets

Find out early what assets are to be transferred in the sale. Ask the buyer what is needed. On your end, you would want to unload all inventory. Prepaid insurance, some supplies, cash, marketable securities, accounts receivable, and the like are not sold. If the buyer does buy your accounts receivables, you will be asked to guarantee collection. The assets most commonly purchased are merchandise inventory, sales and office supplies, fixtures and equipment, and goodwill.

2. Goodwill

Goodwill arises from the special advantages connected with the store — its good name, its credibility with suppliers, capable staff, financial standing, established selling lines, steady buying clientele, and, of course, good location. Goodwill is calculated by capitalizing average net earnings (see capitalized value). The difference between the sale price and the value of physical assets is goodwill.

Goodwill can also be calculated by capitalizing average excess earnings. This method recognizes both earnings and asset contributions. It computes what would be a fair return on the value of assets. If estimated future earnings are higher than this, fair return on the difference of the two figures is capitalized at a higher rate. The amount obtained is considered goodwill.

Add this goodwill figure to the value of assets. The determination of goodwill usually reflects the value of profits above the normal rate of return, i.e., excess profits. But most small businesses do not show a profit (at least in the Profit and Loss statement). They usually show nominal profits or none at all. Often the seller makes an offer that seems fair and negotiations go from there.

3. Inventory

Inventory is usually determined by a physical count. Procedures on the count should be determined beforehand. It is easy to omit items, so take care, because you are more vulnerable than the buyer.

After the count, a value must be put on each item. Most often last cost is used. If there are any doubts about price, a fair bargaining session can solve the problem. Make sure two copies of the inventory are made.

Example:

	1979	1980	1981	1982	1983
Your past sales	257M	340M	355M	367M	390M
% increase		32%	4%	3%	6%

	1984	1985	1986	1987	1988
Your sales forecast	407M	425M	443M	462M	482M
Average % increase	4.3%				

In a case like this where 1980 sales are over 1979 by 32%, probably because of the momentum of the first year's performance, the increase is usually ignored when forecasting future sales. The average increase of the other years worked out to be 4.3%. Use that percentage to project the other years with some rounding up or down.

FIVE YEAR OPERATING STATEMENT

	1979	1980	1981	1982	1983
Sales ($M)	257	340	355	367	390
Cost of goods sold	154	204	213	220	234
Gross margin	103	136	142	147	156
Operating expense*	80	106	112	110	123
PROFIT	23	30	30	37	33

Projected operating statement for the next year can now be made by both buyer and seller.

PROJECTED OPERATING STATEMENT FOR 1984

	SELLER	BUYER
Sales ($M)	407	403
Cost of goods	244	254
Gross margin	153	149
Operating expense*	119	118
PROFIT	34	31

---

*Including owner's salary of $20M

Assume that Total Salable Assets are $112M, appraised and agreed by both parties, then how much should the fair offer be?

If you feel that the buyer's fair return on investment should be capitalized over 5 years, the offer, based on the buyer's anticipated profits of 1984, should be calculated thus:

$$5 \text{ Year} = 20\% \text{ per year}$$

$$\text{Anticipated profits} = \$31M$$

$$\text{Therefore } \$31M \div .20 = \$155M$$

If the negotiations are based on appraised value of assets only, the purchase price would be $112M plus any provision for goodwill.

Since $112M is well below the $155M, negotiations will be necessary. Here are some questions that the buyer might have.

(a) Are assets worth more than the sale price in the light of future sales and potential profits?

(b) Is the risk of the buyer less than anticipated? To pay $155M a reduced risk level will be necessary.

(c) Is the asking price too high? Is it possible for a newcomer to the video business to achieve the sales forecast?

(d) How much goodwill is a fair figure?

(e) What would be an acceptable price for the video store?

f. THE FINAL OFFER

To determine the price, the seller and buyer should sit in a private room with the phone off the hook and no interruptions allowed. Then the process of bargaining begins. Each party will be using psychology on the other to achieve what each thinks is a fair figure.

If you know the buyer has a deadline, time will play a big part in your bargaining position. If you know that the buyer, for some reason, must buy a store by such and such a date, delay negotiation for as long as possible.

If economic conditions are good for the video business, as it now is, your bargaining position is more likely to be strong.

While the negotiations are going on, you must establish that the buyer is creditworthy. The buyer must have enough money or financing in order to pay for the store in full.

g. AFTER THE PRICE IS ESTABLISHED

After the price has been agreed to by both parties, it is time for the buyer to sign a letter of intent stating the monies agreed upon, terms, price, etc. You as a seller must be interested in the following:

(a) The best possible price

(b) Getting the money

(c) Severing liabilities, past and future

(d) Avoiding contract terms and conditions that the buyer may not be able to carry out

The buyer would, on the other hand, be interested in:

(a) Getting a good title at the lowest price

(b) Favorable payment terms

(c) Warranty protection against false statements of the seller, inaccurate financial data, and undisclosed potential liabilities

(d) An indemnification agreement and security deposit

(e) An agreement that you will give some territorial protection — that you will not establish a similar business in the same trading area at a later date

Of course you will engage a lawyer to look after your interests and your buyer will also do the same.

I strongly recommend that you see your accountant about tax and investment matters after you have the money from the sale.

APPENDIX 1

THE 200 MOST POPULAR MOVIES

The following is a list of 200 of the best selling and/or rental titles that I recommend for your store. In some cases, these titles may not be available in both tape and disk formats.

In my opinion, 200 titles is inadequate for starting in the movie rental business today. The minimum number of titles in a new store should be between 800 and 1,000. With that number of titles, you can be competitive in the video rental market. This list will get you started in your selections.

Absence of Malice	Columbia
Airplane	Paramount
Airplane II	Paramount
Alien	CBS - Fox
Amityville Horror, The	WEA
Amityville II: The Posession	WEA
An Evening with Robin Williams	Paramount
Animal House	MCA
Annie	Columbia
Apocalypse Now	Paramount
Arthur	WEA
Atlantic City	Paramount
Author, Author	CBS - Fox
Beatles, The Compleat	MGM/UA
Being There	CBS - Fox
Best Friends	WEA
Best Little Whorehouse in Texas	MCA
Black Emmanuelle	CBS - Fox
Blade Runner	Embassy
Blazing Saddles	WEA
Boat, The	Columbia
Body Heat	WEA
Border, The	MCA
Breaker, Breaker	Embassy
Butterfly	Vestron
Caddyshack	WEA
Candid Camera	Vestron
Cannery Row	MGM/UA
Car Wash	MCA
Carbon Copy	Embassy
Cat People	MCA
Changeling, The	Vestron
Chariots of Fire	WEA
Cheech and Chong's Next Movie	MCA
Cheech and Chong's Up in Smoke	Columbia
Class of 84	Vestron
Clockwork Orange	WEA
Coal Miner's Daughter	MCA
Conan, the Barbarian	MCA
Concrete Jungle, The	Columbia

Deathtrap	WEA
Deathwish II	WEA
Diner	MGM/UA
Dragonslayer	Paramount
Earthling, The	Vestron
Eddie Macon's Run	MCA
Elephant Man, The	Paramount
Emmanuelle	Columbia
Emmanuelle, Joys of a Woman	Paramount
Enigma	Embassy
Escape from Alcatraz	Paramount
Evilspeak	CBS - Fox
Excalibur	WEA
Exorcist	WEA
Exorcist II: The Heretic	WEA
Eye for an Eye	Embassy
Eye of the Needle	CBS - Fox
Fast Times at Ridgemont High	MCA
Final Conflict: Omen III	CBS - Fox
Final Countdown, The	Vestron
Firefox	WEA
First Blood	Thorn - EMI
Fist of Fury	CBS - Fox
For Your Eyes Only	CBS - Fox
Force 10 from Navarone	WEA
Fort Apache, The Bronx	Vestron
48 Hours	Paramount
Frances	Thorn - EMI
Friday the 13th	Paramount
Friday the 13th, Part II	Paramount
Friday the 13th, Part III	Paramount
Gallipoli	Paramount
Game of Death	CBS - Fox
Ghostkeeper	Video-Ville
Ghost Story	MCA
Go Tell the Spartans	Vestron
Good Guys Wear Black	Vestron

Title	Distributor
Halloween	Media
Halloween II	MCA
Halloween III	MCA
Hardcore	Columbia
High Road to China	WEA
History of the World, Part I	CBS - Fox
Hobbit, The	MGM/UA
Honky Tonk Man	WEA
Howling, The	Embassy
I Ought to be n Pictures	CBS - Fox
I, The Jury	CBS - Fox
If You Could See What I Hear	Vestron
Jane Fonda's Workout	WEA
Jaws	MCA
Jaws II	MCA
Kiss Me Goodbye	CBS - Fox
Kentucky Fried Movie	Media
Kramer vs Kramer	Columbia
Last Unicorn	CBS - Fox
Liar's Moon	Vestron
Lipstick	Paramount
Lord of the Rings	Thorn - EMI
Lords of Discipline, The	Paramount
Mad Max	Vestron
Maniac	Media
M.A.S.H. — Goodbye, Farewell and Amen	CBS - Fox
McCartney, Paul — Rockshow	Thorn - EMI
Meatballs	Paramount
Mephisto	VIF
Midsummer Night's Sex Comedy	WEA
Missing	MCA
Missionary, The	Thorn - EMI
Monsignor	CBS - Fox
Moonlighting	MCA
Moonraker	CBS - Fox
Motherlode	Vestron
My Bodyguard	CBS - Fox
My Favorite Year	MGM/UA
National Lampoon's Class Reunion	Vestron
Neighbors	Columbia
Nice Dreams	Columbia
Night Shift	WEA
1941	MCA
Octagon, The	Media
Octopussy	MGM/UA
Officer and A Gentleman, An	Paramount
Omen, The	CBS - Fox
Omen II: Damien	CBS - Fox
On Golden Pond	
Partners	Paramount
Pennies From Heaven	MGM/UA
Pirates of Penzance, The	MCA
Playboy Video Volume I	CBS - Fox
Playboy Video Volume II	CBS - Fox
Playboy Video Volume III	CBS - Fox
Playmate Review	CBS - Fox
Poltergeist	MGM/UA
Porky's	Astral
Postman Always Rings Twice	MGM/UA
Private Eyes, The	Vestron
Private Lessons	MCA
Prize Fighter, The	Media
Quest for Fire	CBS - Fox
Ragtime	Paramount
Red Foxx: Video in a Plain Brown Wrapper	Vestron
Richard Pryor Live Concert	Vestron
Richard Pryor: Live on Sunset Strip	Columbia
Road Warrior, The	WEA
Rock 'n Roll High School	WEA
Rocky	CBS - Fox
Rocky II	CBS - Fox
Rocky III	CBS - Fox
Rolling Stones: Let's Spend the Night Together	Embassy
S.O.B.	MGM/UA
Savannah Smiles	Embassy
Scanners	CBS - Fox
Secret of Nimh, The	MGM/UA
Secret Policeman's Other Ball	MGM/UA
Sharky's Machine	WEA
Shining, The	WEA
Shoot the Moon	MGM/UA
Six Weeks	Columbia
Soldier, The	Embassy
Some Kind of Hero	Paramount
Sophie's Choice	CBS - Fox
Star Trek: The Movie	Paramount
Star Trek II	Paramount
Star Wars	CBS - Fox
Still of the Night	CBS - Fox
Still Smokin'	Paramount
Sting, The	MCA
Sting II	MCA
Stir Crazy	Columbia
Stripes	Columbia
Superman	WEA
Superman II	WEA
Sword and the Sorcerer	MCA
Taps	CBS - Fox
Taxi Driver	Columbia
Tempest	Columbia
Terry Fox Story, The	Astral
Tex	Disney
Texas Chainsaw Massacre	Astral
That Championship Season	MGM/UA
Thing, The	MCA
This is Elvis	WEA
Threshold	Pan-Canada
Time Rider	Pacific Arts
Toy, The	Columbia
Trail of the Pink Panther	CBS - Fox
Tron	Disney

Used Cars	Columbia	You Only Live Twice	CBS - Fox
		Young Doctors in Love	Vestron
Verdict, The	CBS - Fox		
Vice Squad	Embassy	Zapped	Embassy
Victor/Victoria	MGM/UA	Zorro, The Gay Blade	CBS - Fox
Videodrome	MCA		
Wanderers, The	WEA		
WHO Rocks America	CBS - Fox		
Winter Kills	Embassy		
World According to Garp	WEA		

APPENDIX 2

RECOMMENDED MAGAZINES AND BOOKS

a. MAGAZINES

Billboard (Weekly newspaper for trade)
One Astor Plaza
1515 Broadway
New York, NY 10036

Good gossipy section on video; also publishes weekly top rating video cassettes.

Consumer Electronics Monthly (Trade)
325 East 75th Street
New York, NY 10021

Very up-to-date on news about the electronics industry.

Creative Computing (Consumer)
P.O. Box 5214
Boulder, CO 80321

An excellent computer magazine; lots of advertising.

Electronic Games Magazine (Consumer)
P.O. Box 1128
Dover, NJ 07801

Well prepared periodical with informative articles and reviews about video games.

Home Video (Consumer)
475 Park Avenue South
New York, NY 10016

A pretty good magazine that is growing along with the growth of the video business.

Marketnews (Trade)
Hunter Nichols Publishing Ltd.
2282 Queen Street East
Toronto, ON
M4E 1G6

A Canadian trade magazine for the electronics industry.

Sight & Sound Marketing (Trade)
51 East 42nd Street
New York, NY 10017

A trade magazine on stereo and video

Video Advisor (Trade)
P.O. Box 68064
Seattle, WA 98168

An impartial newsletter with good reviews and news; illustrations are poor.

Video Business (Trade)
135 West 50th Street
New York, NY 10020

One of the best in the business — a must for subscription.

Video Magazine (Consumer)
P.O. Box 1117
Dover, NJ 07801

A good video magazine with reviews and up-to-date news of the industry.

Video Mania (Consumer)
P.O. Box 242, Station A
Weston, ON
M9N 3M7

A Canadian magazine that concentrates on Canadian happenings.

Video Review (Consumer)
Viare Publications
350 East 81st Street
New York, NY 10028

A good consumer magazine, lots of reviews on hardware and movies.

Video Scene (Consumer)
Calder Publications (1980) Ltd.
542 Mt. Pleasant Road, Ste. 303
Toronto, ON
M4S 2M7

A Canadian publication that is getting better.

Video Store: The Journal of Video Retailing (Trade)
P.O. Box 19531
Irvine, CA 92713

An excellent trade magazine; it is well distributed.

b. BOOKS

A Practial Introduction to Business
Harold Koontz and Robert M. Fulmer
Richard D. Irwin Inc., Homewood, Illinois

Buying and Selling a Small Business
Michael M. Coltman
International Self-Counsel Press Ltd., Vancouver, B.C.

Getting Sales: A Practical Guide
Richard D. Smith and Ginger Dick
International Self-Counsel Press Ltd., Vancouver, B.C.

Halliwell's Film Guide
Leslie Halliwell
Granada Press, New York

The Home Video Handbook
Charles Bensinger
Video-Info Publications, Santa Fe, New Mexico

How to Interview and Hire Productive People
Jack, Peter and Don McQuaig
Frederick Fell Publishers, New York

How to Sell Anything to Anybody
Joe Girard
Warner Books, New York

Movies on TV (1982-1983 Editions)
Stephen H. Schener
Bantam Books, New York

1981-82 TV Movies
Leonard Martin
Signet, New York

Rating the Movies for Home Video, TV & Cable
Jay A. Brown
Beekman House, New York

The Video Tape and Disc Guide to Home Entertainment
Bookwise Service, Surrey, UK

You Can Negotiate Anything
Herb Cohen
Bantam Books, New York

AMERICAN ORDER FORM

SELF-COUNSEL SERIES
4/83

NATIONAL TITLES

___	Assertiveness for Managers	8.95
___	Basic Accounting for the Small Business	4.50
___	Collection Techniques for the Small Business	4.95
___	Exporting from the U.S.A.	12.95
___	Financial Control for the Small Business	5.50
___	Financial Freedom on $5 a Day	5.95
___	Fundraising for Non-Profit Groups	5.50
___	Franchising in the U.S.	5.95
___	The Future of Money	2.95
___	Getting Sales	14.95
___	Immigrating to Canada	9.95
___	Immigrating to the U.S.A.	12.95
___	Learn to Type	6.50
___	The Money Spinner	14.95
___	Resort Condos & Time Sharing	4.50
___	Retirement in the Pacific Northwest	4.95
___	Runaway Inflation	2.95
___	Starting a Successful Business on West Coast	12.95
___	You and the Police	3.50
___	Word Processing	8.95
___	Working Couples	4.50

STATE TITLES
Please indicate which state edition is required.

___ Consumer Rights
    ☐ Washington 4.50 ☐ Oregon 3.50

___ Divorce Guide
    ☐ Washington 7.95 Oregon 8.95

___ Incorporation and Business Guide
    ☐ Washington 9.95 ☐ Oregon 9.95

___ Landlord/Tenant Rights
    ☐ Washington 4.50 ☐ Oregon 6.95

___ Marriage and Family Law
    ☐ Washington 4.50 ☐ Oregon 4.95

___ Probate Guide
    ☐ Washington 9.95

___ Real Estate Buying/Selling Guide
    ☐ Washington 5.95 ☐ Oregon 3.95

___ Small Claims Court
    ☐ Washington 4.50

___ Wills
    ☐ Washington 3.95

___ Will and Estate Planning for Oregon
    ☐ Oregon 4.95

PACKAGED FORMS

___ Probate
    ☐ Washington 6.50

___ Will and Estate Planning Kit

___ Incorporation
    ☐ Washington 11.95 ☐ Oregon 10.50

___ Divorce
    ☐ Washington 9.95

    ☐ Oregon Set A (Petitioner) 12.95
    ☐ Oregon Set B (Co-Petitioners) 12.95

___ If You Love Me — Put It In Writing 7.95

All prices subject to change without notice.

Please send orders to:

SELF-COUNSEL PRESS INC.
1303 N. Northgate Way
Seattle, Washington 98133
Phone: (206) 522-8383

☐ Check here for free catalog

(PLEASE PRINT)

NAME _____

ADDRESS _____

CITY _____

STATE _____

ZIP CODE _____

Check or Money Order enclosed. ☐

If order is under $20, add $1.50 for postage and handling.

CANADIAN ORDER FORM
SELF-COUNSEL SERIES

6/83

NATIONAL TITLES:

Adopted?	3.95
Advertising for Small Business	4.95
Assertiveness for Managers	8.95
Basic Accounting	4.50
Becoming a Canadian	3.50
Better Book for Getting Hired	8.95
Changing Your Name in Canada	3.50
Civil Rights in Canada	6.50
Collection Techniques for the Small Business	4.95
Credit, Debt, and Bankruptcy	5.95
Criminal Procedure in Canada	11.95
Drinking and Driving	4.50
Editing Your Newsletter	14.95
Energy, Money & Your Future	4.95
Exporting	12.50
Federal Incorporation and Business Guide	11.95
Financial Control for the Small Business	5.50
Financial Freedom on $5 A Day	5.95
For Sale By Owner	3.50
Franchising in Canada	5.95
Fundraising	5.50
Future of Money	2.95
Getting Money	14.95
Getting Sales	14.95
Getting Started	11.95
How You Too Can Make a Million... In the Mail Order Business	7.95
Immigrating to Canada	9.95
Immigrating to the U.S.A.	12.95
Importing	21.95
Insuring Business Risks	3.50
Learn to Type	6.50
Life Insurance for Canadians	3.50
Media Law Handbook	5.95
Mike Grenby's Tax Tips	5.50
Mike Grenby's Money Book	5.50
Money Spinner	14.95
Mortgage and Foreclosure Handbook	5.95
Public Speaking	4.95
Resort Condos	4.50
Runaway Inflation	2.95
Retirement Guide for Canadians	7.95
Starting a Successful Business in Canada	12.95
Tax Law Handbook	11.95
Taxpayer Alert!	4.95
Tax Shelters in Canada	5.95
Trusts and Trust Companies	3.95
War on Gold	4.95
Word Processing	8.95
Working Couples	4.50
Write Right!	(Paper) 4.95
	(Cloth) 5.95

PROVINCIAL TITLES:
Please indicate which provincial edition is required.

Consumer Book
□B.C. 7.95 □Ontario 6.95

Divorce Guide
□B.C. 9.95 □Alberta 7.95 □Ontario 9.95 □Man./Sask. 7.95

Employee/Employer Rights
□B.C. 5.95 □Alberta 2.95 □Ontario 5.50

Marriage & Family Law
□B.C. 6.95 □Alberta 5.95 □Ontario 6.95

Fight That Ticket
□B.C. 4.95 □Alberta 2.95 □Ontario 3.95

Incorporation Guide
□B.C. 12.95 □Alberta 14.95 □Ontario 12.95 □Man./Sask. 9.95

Landlord/Tenant Rights
□B.C. 4.95 □Alberta 5.50 □Ontario 5.95

Real Estate Guide
□B.C. 6.95 □Alberta 4.95 □Ontario 6.50

Small Claims Court Guide
□B.C. 5.95 □Alberta 2.50 □Ontario 4.95

Probate Guide
□B.C. 12.95 □Alberta 9.95 □Ontario 9.95

Wills
□B.C. 4.95 □Alberta 5.50 □Ontario 4.95

Wills/Probate Procedure
□Sask./Man. 4.95

PACKAGED FORMS:

Incorporation
□B.C. 12.50 □Alberta 11.95 □Ontario 14.95
□Man./Sask. 7.95 □Federal 9.95
□Minute Books 16.50

Divorce
□B.C. 10.95 □Alberta 12.95 □Ontario 14.50 □Man. 8.50 □Sask. 12.50

Probate
□B.C. Administration 14.95 □B.C. Probate 13.95 □Alberta 12.95 □Ontario 15.50

Sell Your Own Home
□B.C. 4.95 □Alberta 3.95 □Ontario 4.95

Rental Form Kit (B.C., Alberta, Ontario, Man./Sask.) ... 4.50
Have You Made Your Will? ... 5.95
If You Love Me Put It In Writing   Contract Kit ... 9.95
If You Leave Me Put It In Writing   B.C. Separation Agreement Kit ... 14.95

NOTE: *All prices subject to change without notice.*

Books are available in book and department stores, or use the order form below.

Please enclose Cheque or Money Order (plus sales tax where applicable) or give us your Mastercard or Visa number (please include expiry date).

(PLEASE PRINT)

Name _____

Address _____

City _____

Province _____ Postal Code _____

□ Visa / □ Mastercard _____ Expiry Date _____

If order is under $20.00, add $1.00 for postage and handling.

Please send orders to: □ Check here for free catalogue.

INTERNATIONAL SELF-COUNSEL PRESS LTD.
306 West 25th Street
North Vancouver, British Columbia
V7N 2G1